How to
Communicate Successfully

Also by Andrew Wright

In this series:
How to Enjoy Paintings
How to be Entertaining
How to Improve Your Mind
How to be a Successful Traveller

with David Betteridge and Michael Buckby:
Games for Language Learning

with Michael Beaumont:
Teacher's Guide to the How to . . . readers

Pictures for Language Learning

with Penny Ur:
Five–Minute Activities

How to Communicate Successfully

Andrew Wright

with drawings by the author

CAMBRIDGE
UNIVERSITY PRESS

Published by the Press Syndicate of the University of Cambridge
The Pitt Building, Trumpington Street, Cambridge CB2 1RP
40 West 20th Street, New York, NY 10011–4211, USA
10 Stamford Road, Oakleigh, Melbourne 3166, Australia

© Cambridge University Press 1987

First published 1987
Fifth printing 1995

Printed in Malta by
Interprint Limited

ISBN 0 521 27547 4

SE

Contents

Thanks

I would like to thank Alison Silver, the editor of this series, who has made a significant contribution to each book in terms of content and presentation. I would also like to thank Monica Vincent for her valuable advice, Peter Donovan for his support during the long period of writing and Peter Ducker for his concern for the design and typography. I am also grateful to the teachers and students of Nord Anglia for trying out samples of the texts and giving me useful advice for their improvement.

In a book of this kind one is naturally influenced by a large number of writers, lecturers, friends and acquaintances. However, I should like to acknowledge the following writers and their books in particular: J. M. and M. J. Cohen, *Modern Quotations*, Penguin; *The Oxford Dictionary of Quotations*, Oxford University Press; *The International Thesaurus of Quotations*, Penguin; Osgood, Suci and Tannenbaum for their test on page 8; Colin Cherry, *World Communication, Threat or Promise?*, Wiley Interscience; Basil Bernstein, 'Elaborated and restricted codes: their social origins and some consequences', in K. Danziger, *Readings in Child Socialization*, Pergamon Press; L. Carmichael et al, *Journal of Experimental Psychology* Vol. 15; I. Eibl-Eibesfeldt, 'The expressive behaviour of the deaf and blind born', in Von Cranach and Vine (eds), *Non-Verbal Behaviour and Expressive Movements*, Academic Press; Thomas A. Harris, *I'm OK, You're OK*, Pan; Muriel James and Dorothy Jongeward, *Born to Win*, Addison Wesley; Julius Fast, *Body Language*, Pan; Desmond Morris, *Manwatching*, Triad Panther; Desmond Morris et al, *Gestures, their origins and distribution*, Jonathan Cape Ltd; Gerard Nierenberg and Henry Calero, *How to Read a Person Like a Book*, Heinrich Hanau Publications; E. Hall, 'The Anthropology of Manners', *Scientific American* Vol. 192; S. Jourard, 'An exploratory study of body accessibility', *British Journal of Social and Clinical Psychology* Vol. 5; Pastor Lavater, *Physiognomische Fragmente zur Beförderung der Menschenkenntnis und Menschenliebe*; Eric Berne, *Games People Play*, Penguin; Gary T. Hunt, *Public Speaking*, Prentice Hall; Philip R. Lund, *Compelling Selling*, Macmillan; Philip J. Koerper, *How to Talk Your Way to Success in Selling*, Parker Publishing; Michael Argyle and Peter Trower, *Person to Person*, Harper & Row.

About this book

How to Communicate Successfully is one in a series of five books. There are seven chapters, each dealing with a different aspect of communicating. There are several different sections in each chapter, and some may be more interesting and relevant to you than others. There is no need to read every section. I hope you will find it all interesting and entertaining, and that your reading of English will improve as well as your communicating.

★ Indicates that there is a question you should think about on your own.
★★ Indicates that if you are reading the book with another person you should talk about this particular question with him or her.

You may be reading the book while studying English in a class, with a teacher, or you may be reading it at home in the evenings, or on a train, or anywhere else – it doesn't matter!

What I do hope is that you enjoy reading about communicating successfully – in English!

A MAN BECOMES THE CREATURE OF UNIFORM

Some thoughts about communicating

★ Do you agree with any of them?

Good clothes open all doors.

(Thomas Fuller, *Gnomologia*, 1732)

A man becomes the creature of uniform.

(Napoleon I, *Maxims*, 1804–15)

A lady wants to be dressed exactly like everybody else but she gets pretty upset if she sees anybody else dressed exactly like her.

(Ogden Nash, *Marriage Lines*, 1964)

Only connect!

(E.M. Forster, *Howards End*, 1910)

To think justly, we must understand what others mean: to know the value of our thoughts, we must try their effect on other minds.

(William Hazlitt, *The Plain Speaker*, 1826)

When the eyes say one thing, and the tongue another, a practised man relies on the language of the first.

(Emerson, *The Conduct of Life*, 1860)

The only way to have a friend is to be one.

(Emerson, 'Friendship,' *Essays: First Series*, 1841)

Friends show their love in times of trouble, not in happiness.

(Euripides, *Orestes*, 408 BC)

One loyal friend is worth ten thousand relatives.

(Euripides, *Orestes*, 408 BC)

It is in the thirties that we want friends. In the forties we know they won't save us any more than love did.

(F. Scott Fitzgerald, 'Note-Books,' *The Crack-Up*, 1945)

A good friend is my nearest relation.

(Thomas Fuller, *Gnomologia*, 1732)

Friends are born, not made.

(Henry Adams, *The Education of Henry Adams*, 1907)

Wishing to be friends is quick work, but friendship is a slow-ripening fruit.

(Aristotle, *Nicomachean Ethics*, 4th c. BC)

Talk does not cook rice.

(Chinese Proverb)

Your friend is the man who knows all about you, and still likes you.

(Elbert Hubbard, *The Note Book*, 1927)

It's no good trying to keep up old friendships. It's painful for both sides. The fact is, one grows out of people, and the only thing is to face it.

(W. Somerset Maugham, *Cakes and Ale*, 1930)

The friendship that can come to an end never really began.

(Publilius Syrus, *Moral Sayings*, 1st c. BC)

Only connect!

The English word 'communicate' comes from the Latin word 'communicare'. It means 'to give' or 'to share'. And, most commonly today, it means to give or share information and ideas. 'Communicate' can mean 'talk together', 'discuss', 'consult' and 'tell'. We may communicate in order to cooperate with others or in order to attract them, persuade them, organise them or control them . . .

The *Oxford English Dictionary* also says that 'communicate' means 'to have a common door with'. The two people in this photograph know each other; they speak the same language (even the

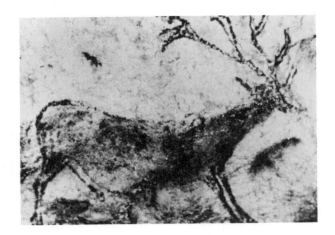

Lascaux cave painting. Photograph by Ray Delvert, © DACS 1985.

same local language), they share the same history, similar experiences and similar values. They can talk and usually understand each other. There is an open door between them. And, indeed, this type of door encourages people to communicate.

This book is about opening doors between people.

WE'LL HUNT TONIGHT

The paintings in the cave at Lascaux in the Dordogne region of France are about 20,000 years old. Most of the pictures show animals; deer, bison and horses. These were the animals which the people hunted.

If 20 or 30 people are going to hunt they must organise themselves. They have to be able to give each other information quickly during the hunt. They have to be able to ask for information. And they will probably want to encourage each other and talk about their experiences afterwards.

The hunters at Lascaux certainly used gestures as well. Perhaps they crept up on the animals and signalled to each other to move, to lie quietly, to race ahead. And perhaps some of them

wore special clothing or headdresses in order to show who were the leaders. Words, gestures and clothing are all important aspects of communication.

Successful communication is essential for our survival. We need language as much today as we did 20,000 years ago . . . perhaps more!

WORDS, GESTURES AND CLOTHING

We look and listen for meaning. We may not always realise that we understand as much by looking as by listening to other people.

THE CHILDREN WHO COULDN'T SPEAK

If there are no people around us we don't learn how to communicate. There have been several cases where children have been discovered, unable to speak a human language, after years of living alone or with animals. We don't know, of course, whether the children who lived with animals were able to communicate with them, but when they were discovered they certainly couldn't communicate with humans.

In 1798 a teenager was found in the woods at Aveyron in France. He had lived alone in the woods since he was a small child, and he was unable to speak.

In 1920, in India, two young girls were found living in the wilds. People said that wolves had looked after them. They couldn't speak.

In 1970 a boy called Genie was found

Gazelle boy discovered

IT IS reported that a boy was found living with gazelles in the Syrian desert by Bedouins who were hunting gazelles in a jeep.

They claimed that he was running at over 80 kilometres an hour and was faster than the jeep. He could only make animal sounds and lived on roots, grass and water.

When he was captured he was taken to a lunatic asylum in Damascus where he ran around the garden, plucking and eating grass and drinking water from a stream. It is thought that his mother abandoned him in the Syrian desert.

The picture shows him (he is about 14 years old) with his hands and feet tied to prevent his escape in the stony desert wastes near Damascus.

in a room. He was 14 and he had been living alone in the room since he was 14 months old. The people who were responsible for him had given him very little food and had never talked to him. Genie had to learn how to speak when he was taken away from these people.

In 1976 a boy was found in the forests of Burundi in central Africa. He had been living with monkeys; he walked on his hands and feet and climbed like a monkey. He couldn't speak.

PEOPLE WHO CAN'T UNDERSTAND

Speaking and understanding are complicated even if you have been brought up in a home rather than in a desert. We might know a language very well but can we always express ourselves so that the other person can understand what we are trying to communicate?

CHECKLIST FOR SUCCESSFUL COMMUNICATION

Can he or she hear me?
Can he or she understand the words?
Is he or she interested?

Can he or she see me?
Does he or she understand the expression on my face and the gestures I am making?
Does he or she understand my behaviour? (For example, raising my glass of beer and saying, 'Cheers!')
Does he or she want to look at me?

If the answer to any of the questions above is NO you will probably fail to communicate.

How to use verbal language

Why do we want to communicate?

★ Think of some of the times you have tried to communicate today. Why did you communicate? What were your reasons?

Here is a list of some of the main reasons for communicating. Look through the list and see if you can remember an example of each from your day.

Giving or asking for factual information
Did you give or ask for factual information today?

Expressing what you think or finding out what someone else thinks
Have you told somebody what you think or asked somebody what they think today? Perhaps you agreed or disagreed with something which someone did or said. You may have denied something. You may have offered to do something. Perhaps you told someone that you were able to do something. You may have said that you were sure of something or that you weren't sure of something. You may have asked for permission to do something or you may have given someone permission to do something.

Expressing what you feel and finding out what someone else feels
Have you expressed pleasure, displeasure, liking, not liking, satisfaction or dissatisfaction, disappointment, worry, sympathy, gratitude, or desire today?

Expressing what you think is right or wrong
Have you done that today and did you find out what the other person thinks?

Apologising to or forgiving someone
Have you apologised to anyone today?

Organising someone
Have you suggested what someone might do? Or advised them to do something? Or asked them to do something? Have you ordered them to do something?

Being sociable
Have you greeted people or said goodbye today? Perhaps you have introduced people to each other?

Why is he speaking?

★ What is A's reason for speaking in each case? (See answers on page 82.)

But he doesn't mean what he says!

People often say one thing but mean something else. We might use the language of 'giving information' but we

may simply want to be friendly. (Or we may want to give information and be friendly!) Here are some people having conversations.

★ What do you think they might be saying and thinking? (See suggested answers on page 82.)

We all think one thing and say another
. . . sometimes. Is this necessarily bad?

Words! Words! Words!

What does the word 'mother' mean to you? In the dictionary it says 'a female parent'. But doesn't the word mean much more than that to you?

★★ Would another person have the same associations? How many of your associations with 'mother' would be similar to those of people who live in another country?

We can all agree about the dictionary meaning. But how often is the word 'mother' used only to communicate that biological relationship? We

connect many experiences and values with the words we use. And if the person you are talking to has different connections he or she will not understand what you mean, at least, not exactly. And so you fail to communicate.

People who speak the same language may misunderstand each other. A foreigner to your country may know the dictionary definition of the words you are using but not understand what you mean. And, of course, the same may happen to you when you visit another country.

Here are some words. Don't look up their meanings in a dictionary but try to decide what they mean for you. What experiences have you had which give the word a 'personal' meaning for you? For example, for me the word 'hen' means: a friendly sound; the sight of a hen on hot dusty ground; collecting eggs while they are still warm.

★★ Compare your meaning for these words with a friend's meaning:
country   friend   valuable
happy   kind   mirror   morning
moon   car   television   news

★★ Here is another test. Do the test and ask your friends to do it as well. Then see if you have similar associations with the words. Two adjectives are given and you have to decide which one is true for you. You can mark a point anywhere between the two adjectives. For example: what do you think of the verb 'to study'?

good ... ... bad
A lazy or uninterested student might place the mark like this ...
good ... ... **X** bad
I am sure you will put your mark like this ...
good **X** ... ... bad

Think of the verb 'to study' again. Where are you going to put your mark between these adjectives to express your feelings about the idea of studying?

good ... ... bad
calm ... ... excitable
feminine ... ... masculine
ugly ... ... beautiful
fast ... ... slow
true ... ... false
light ... ... heavy
active ... ... passive
hard ... ... soft

Now join your marks. The line you have drawn is your profile for the verb 'to study'. You can now compare your profile with your friends' profiles.

DOES 'CH'A' MEAN 'TEA'?

Most British people like to have milk in their tea. If they go to China and ask for a cup of tea they will get a shock! The cup will be small and it won't have a handle . . . and the tea won't have milk in it! 'Ch'a' in Chinese doesn't mean 'tea' in English. Well, not exactly! However, this isn't really a serious difference. The British visitor soon learns the difference in meaning. But the associations which a British person has with tea and the associations a Chinese person has with tea will be different as well. And these will be very much more difficult to learn. For example, a British person may associate comfort and relaxation with tea whereas a Chinese may at least partly associate it with more formal customs and ceremonies.

We don't seem to speak the same language!

The generation gap

People of 40 usually have different interests, concerns and worries to people of 20. They may also have different ideas on what is valuable and what is right and wrong. These are aspects of the generation gap. People of different generations may even use different words for some things.

★ Think of someone you know from a different generation. Can you think of any words which he or she doesn't know? Do they know the meaning of any words that you don't know?

An English school student (in Manchester) explained the meaning of these words to me.

sound = good   'Last night was really sound.'

brill = brilliant, good (*Sound* and *brill* are more or less the same in meaning.)

tight = nasty and mean   'He's really tight to his little sister.'

slag off = criticise   'She slagged him off because he was late again.'

poser = someone who thinks they look good and wants to show it

weirdo = someone of the same generation who behaves very individually

trendy = daring and fashionable (not just fashionable)

square = someone who is conventional, ordinary and boring

sap = square

dead = very   'He's dead brill.' 'She's dead tight.'

The knowledge gap

People who share similar experiences and interests often develop their own language. This language helps them to communicate better and, at the same time, makes it more difficult for other people to take part.

Here is an extract from the Collins *Gem Dictionary of Basic Facts on Computers*. Computers are a new technology and a new language has been developed to talk about them. If we simply read these definitions we won't learn very much. Without knowledge and experience the words will remain meaningless.

Instruction This is part of a computer program and it is the part that tells the computer what it should be doing at that stage. For example: Print or Add.

Instruction Address Register This **register** stores in turn the **addresses** of the instructions that the computer has to carry out. If during a program you could look inside this register you would find that it contained the address of the next instruction.

Insulator A material that has a very high resistance to electric current so that the current flow through it is negligible. One of the best insulators known is silicon dioxide which is created on the surface of silicon by heating.

Integrated Circuit A **solid state** circuit in which all the components are formed upon a single piece of **semiconductor** material. The first one consisted of a transistor and a resistor and was created in 1959. Since then the number of components on a 'chip' has nearly doubled each year. LSI (large scale integration) means an integrated circuit with more than 100 **logic gates** or over 1000 memory **bits**.

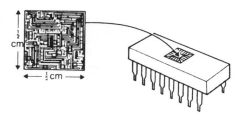

Intelligent Terminal A terminal which retains a program and allows processing of **data** to be carried out without further access to the computer.

Interface This is the circuitry (or **hardware**) needed between two devices so that they can be connected together. Such a circuit board might compensate for differences in speed-of-working or transmission speeds or might translate the codes. Often it is the type of transmission that has to be changed and the interface is attached inside one of the devices.

We expect specialists to know things that we don't know. And we expect them to develop new ideas. For both reasons we must expect specialists to use new words or to use words in new ways. If, however, someone uses a new word to make an old idea seem new and to make the rest of us feel stupid then we should protest!

The Arabic language has many words which refer to the camel. An Eskimo would probably not really understand any of them unless he lived and worked with camels in the desert. On the other hand, the Eskimo has about 12 words for snow (snow which is falling, is fresh on the ground, is frozen hard, etc.) and most Arab people would find it difficult to understand these words even if they were explained.

In English there are now over one million words. The average British person knows between 30,000 and 60,000 words. We may speak the same language but we don't necessarily use the same words. If we want to communicate successfully we must share similar experiences as well as the same words.

Characteristics of everyday speech

From your experience would you agree that some people:
- speak in very short sentences
- don't make full sentences
- jump from one bit of an idea to another
- often use personal pronouns like 'he', 'you', etc.
- talk about physical events rather than about abstract ideas or the analysis of events
- assume that the person they are speaking to knows what they are talking about

Here is an example of this way of using language. The speaker is trying to analyse and describe why young people become involved in violent action. How could the ideas be expressed more clearly?

"It's all according like well those
    youths and that if they get with
    gangs and that they most
they most
have a bit of a lark around and
say it goes wrong
and that and they probably knock some
    off
I think they do it just to be big you
    know
getting publicity here and there!"

Of course, there are people who analyse experience and express themselves clearly. Some people are very careful to explain their ideas so that the other person will understand.

Some people want to share more than they want to explain. They don't try to analyse: they prefer to describe their experience of a subject and to add their opinion on it. They believe the person they are talking to will have the same opinion. They often say phrases like, 'Well, it isn't right is it?' 'Well, it's only natural isn't it?'

If someone who likes to analyse speaks to someone who prefers to share, there may be poor communication!

> Well, it's not right, is it?

> Well, it depends on how you look at it.

Language and thinking

Look at each of the pictures below and read the word(s) under them.

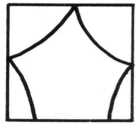

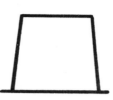

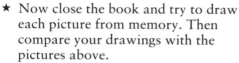

curtains in a window   hat   two

★ Now close the book and try to draw each picture from memory. Then compare your drawings with the pictures above.

Your drawings probably look a little bit more like the objects named than the pictures.

In the original experiment a lot of people were shown the same picture but were given different words. For example, half the people were shown

the first picture above and the words 'curtains in a window', and many of them produced drawings like the one on the left below. And half the people were shown the same picture with the words 'diamond in a rectangle', and many of them produced drawings like the one on the right.

The experiment shows that our perception and our memory are influenced by words.

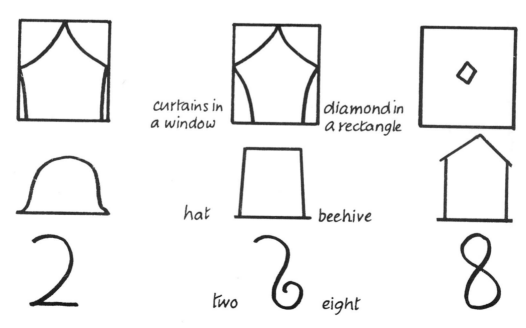

curtains in a window   diamond in a rectangle

hat   beehive

two   eight

Speaking in different ways

What are they saying?

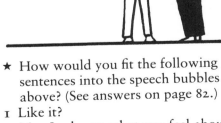

★ How would you fit the following sentences into the speech bubbles above? (See answers on page 82.)

1 Like it?
2 May I ask you what you feel about this painting?
3 I love it.
4 Absolutely agree. Absolutely agree.
5 Excuse me, please. Would you mind if I ask you what you think about this picture?
6 Rather ridiculous, don't you think?
7 What do you think of it?
8 I particularly dislike it.

⟫⟶

9 It's great.

10 I can only express my deepest dislike for it.

In the illustrations the people change but the place remains the same. In order to decide on what to put in the speech bubbles you had to look at the sort of people they are: you looked at their age, their dress, the way they stand and move and the way they behave towards each other. You had to imagine what the relationship is between the people.

If you have similar answers to mine (see page 82) then you have a good sense of the way British people can speak formally or informally. Most languages have formal and informal language; simple examples in English are 'Hi!' and 'Good morning!' A senior official will probably be upset if you say 'Hi!' and your best friend will think you unfriendly if you say 'Good morning!'

★ What are corresponding examples in your own language?

We might spend years learning the grammar and vocabulary of a foreign language, and pass several examinations. We go to the foreign country and . . . disaster! We don't get on with the people! If this happens it might be because we don't speak in the appropriate kind of language. We might be using very informal language in situations requiring very formal language. We can learn how to use the correct degree of formality only by experience. And then only by believing that it is important.

The choice of words and the construction of sentences is important. However, there are some other very important characteristics of spoken language. And if you get these wrong there might be a disaster!

Don't play the wrong music!

A person with a flat, dull voice which neither rises nor falls sounds like a flat and dull person! But they may not be! A person can give the impression that they are bored, indignant, friendly or angry just by the sound of their voice.

A French friend of mine once said to me, 'Your accent in French is excellent but you will never sound like a Frenchman until you put all your heart into your voice. It is a pity because you are a lively person and yet you don't sound lively to a Frenchman!'

We learn the grammar and vocabulary and even the correct pronunciation of the foreign language but we may forget the important emotional effect of the music of our speech. For British people the intonation of some languages is attractive. Unfortunately, the intonation of some other countries can communicate the wrong meaning. British people are sometimes offended because they think the other person is unfriendly even though they have spoken a perfect English sentence! And this failure of communication can also happen between British people. Some British people think the intonation in the Birmingham accent seems to express bored indignation!

If you want to communicate successfully with another person, you may have to think about the music of your own voice. At the same time if you meet someone from a different part of your country or from another country, BE CAREFUL! Don't judge them only by their intonation.

Talking to foreign visitors

I have a friend who is always happy to help foreign visitors. He realises that they may not be able to understand English very well so . . . he speaks in a loud voice and uses what he thinks is a useful foreign accent!

Here is part of a conversation which my friend had with a foreign visitor. He spoke loudly and used his foreign accent but the visitor didn't understand him!

'Haddon Hall . . . most rewarding place to pay a visit. You're sure to be bowled over by it! Most fascinating example of Gothic domestic architecture, you know medieval buildings. It was started in Norman times and then they carried on adding bits right up until the 16th century. Splendid long gallery there. Exquisite ceiling. Don't miss the rose garden either! Very romantic! But don't let it turn your head or you will fall for the first person of the opposite sex that you clap eyes on! Then you will have to settle down here and not go home! Ho! Ho! Where did you say you come from?'

Here are a few tips which will help foreign visitors understand you when you speak in your own language to them:
— use short and complete sentences
— repeat your main points
— don't change from one point to another without any warning
— use simple words, the sort of words which people might know after one or two years of learning your language
— don't use idioms too much, they are often difficult to understand, particularly because they often seem to mean something else
— look and listen carefully to see if they have understood
★ How should my friend have described Haddon Hall? Think of someone who doesn't know as much English as you. Write down how you would describe Haddon Hall to him or her. Then compare your version with the one on page 83. Yours may be different but just as successful.

Here are the meanings of the various idioms and phrasal verbs you may not be familiar with.

to be bowled over: to be overcome by excitement

to carry on: to continue

to turn someone's head: to make someone think they are marvellous or perhaps in this case, become so romantic they can't make a wise judgement

to fall for: to fall in love with

to clap eyes on: see

to settle down: to live in one place

How to understand body language

Look as well as listen!

I CAN READ HIM LIKE A BOOK... OR CAN I?

ARE YOU GOING TO LONDON?

WAITING ROOM

BUFFET

Well cut hair.

Clothes etc.: Shirt. Tie loose. Shirt unbuttoned. A casual, relaxed look.

Position: This shoulder is higher. She is rather stiff and probably protecting herself.

Expression: Her eyebrows are low and together. She's frowning

Position: She is suspicious. Chin up.

Expression: The 'half smile'. Up on one side and down on the other. What is he thinking?

Gesture: He almost snapped his fingers.

Position: She hasn't turned to face him. She doesn't want to acknowledge him.

Position: Elbow and arm back. Hand held casually on hip.

Position: He stands facing her. His legs are apart and straight, feet well apart.

Clothes etc. A fashionable quality suit. A smart leather suitcase.

distance

This distance is about two metres. This is not <u>too</u> near for strangers <u>if</u> the platform is crowded... but it isn't!

Position: Legs together. She isn't relaxed.

Clothes etc. Note travel labels which show that he is widely travelled.

Clothes etc. Expensive and fashionable shoes.

Clothes etc.: Old fashioned but practical suitcase. Is <u>she</u> like that?

Position: Feet pointing inwards. She is probably not a confident person.

Will she accept his advances? No! But why not? His words seem innocent!

★★ Study him. Study her. Decide on your answer and see if a friend agrees with you.

Some psychologists believe that we communicate 65% of our ideas and feelings without words! The shape of our bodies and faces, the movements and gestures we make, the clothes we wear, how near we stand to each other and whether we touch each other . . . all these communicate. And all of these types of information must be studied if we want to understand what the other person is saying.

Brian Roberts isn't a confident person. He isn't confident that he can make friends and he isn't confident that he can be successful in business. He has watched and envied confident people since he was a child. He has noticed that they often seem to be calm; they speak slowly and clearly; they don't hurry. Brian Roberts has learned to move and speak slowly; he smokes a pipe and he smiles, he believes, with a quiet confidence. Some of the information he communicates says, 'I am confident, and a "man of the world"'. But, if other people study all the information, they will know that that isn't the true story at all! He sometimes lifts his head and stretches his neck as if his shirt collar is too tight . . . but it isn't. Sometimes he pats his hair because he thinks it isn't tidy. He often taps his foot. These are signs of the anxious side of Brian Roberts.

★ Do you know anybody who seems to be saying one thing but really is saying another? Do you wear clothes and behave in a way which completely represents you as you really are?

Misunderstood information might lose a friend or some business or might prevent us from seeing the truth about ourselves.

But it's only natural!

People often say that the British are very traditional, and it is probably true. But who isn't traditional? Many years ago I met a student from Germany. She told me she thought that the British are very traditional and she was critical. She obviously felt that she was a modern young woman and was impatient with tradition. I said, 'But you are very traditional!' She was astonished! She said, 'How can you say that?' And I said, 'Because whenever we meet you want to shake hands!' And she replied, 'But it's only natural!'

Some years ago I took a group of very friendly East European people to a small local concert. In fact, it was a parents' evening at a local school. The headteacher who enjoyed playing the piano, contributed to the evening's entertainment by playing music by Debussy. My visitors were very enthusiastic and began a slow handclap to show their appreciation. Unfortunately, a slow handclap is an expression of disgust in Britain. This 'non-verbal' language was completely misunderstood, and the evening was rather difficult after that!

In Greece people often shake their heads from side to side in a rocking motion and mean 'Yes'.

This 'rocking shake' is so similar to the ordinary and worldwide horizontal headshake that many people think it must mean 'No'. A friend of mine told me that when he was in Greece some

years ago he went to a harbour to take a boat to a different island. He asked if the boat had gone and the man replied by shaking his head! My friend thought this meant 'No, the boat hasn't gone.' So he waited for hours!

SOME NON-VERBAL LANGUAGE IS 'NATURAL' AND SOME ISN'T

People laugh, smile, cry and show fear in similar ways all over the world. The psychologist, Eibl-Eibesfeldt, studied a group of children who had been born blind and deaf. He found that they laugh, cry, smile, sulk and show surprise and anger in the same way as other children.

It is true that certain types of crying show unhappiness in every country in the world (some show happiness!). However, the attitude of people to crying is different in different cultures. Traditionally, British males don't cry! If they do cry many people think they are weak. In some cultures if a man is in great distress, it is acceptable and people feel it is 'natural' and right for him to cry.

The head toss

Desmond Morris and his colleagues at the University of Oxford examined the use of 20 different gestures in 40 different places in Europe. The 'head toss' was one of these gestures.

The head is tossed quickly upwards and backwards and then it is lowered again more slowly. The eyebrows are usually raised and often the eyes are rolled back. Sometimes the eyes are closed. The person may make a soft 'click' with his tongue. If the people are standing very close together then the head may not be tossed. The person may raise his eyebrows, roll his eyes upwards and click his tongue. What does the head toss mean to you?

Desmond Morris and his colleagues published their findings in a book called *Gestures, their origins and distribution* (published by Jonathan Cape Ltd). They made various points in their book. Here are some of them:
1 'Many of the gestures had several major meanings.' For example, if someone taps the side of his head what does he mean? He may mean that he thinks that you are intelligent or he may mean that he thinks you are stupid! And this can lead to very unhappy misunderstandings!
2 Most gestures are used in many countries. Very few gestures can be called, for example, 'French' or 'Italian'. However, some of the meanings are special to one country or to one region of a country.
3 Sometimes these regions of a country may be small and part of a much bigger

language area. The reasons for this are historical. Some gestures were left behind by colonialists or other influential foreign 'visitors'.

4 Sometimes a gesture means several different things in one place.

Desmond Morris and his colleagues asked 1,200 people in 40 places whether they used the 'head toss'. 554 said they did not use this gesture. 302 people said they used it and it meant 'No' (or general negation). 314 people used it for other meanings (seven meanings). This means that the 'head toss' is often misunderstood. For example, when British people go on holiday to Italy they are sometimes offended by the 'head toss'. Many British people think that the 'head toss' means that the person thinks that he is superior and that you are rather stupid!

THE HISTORY OF THE HEAD TOSS MEANING 'NO'

Desmond Morris didn't find anybody who used the 'head toss' to mean 'No' in Northern Europe, Spain, Portugal or Tunisia. He found very few people in the north of Italy or in Sardinia who used the gesture in this way. However, 96% of the people in the south of Italy used the 'head toss' to mean 'No'. Why

is this? Morris believes that the 'head toss' meaning 'No' was left behind by the Greeks 2,000 years ago! The Greeks traded with Southern Italy, they founded cities, for example, 'Neapolis' (new city) which became 'Naples'. Although the Romans eventually took control of the region the local people never stopped using the 'head toss' to mean 'No'.

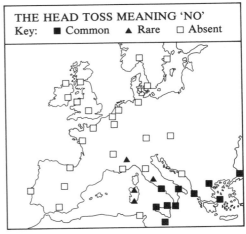

THE HEAD TOSS MEANING 'NO'
Key: ■ Common ▲ Rare □ Absent

THE TRUE AND AUTHENTIC HEAD TOSS!

In the research done by Desmond Morris there were seven other meanings given for the 'head toss':
– beckon ('Come on.' 'This way.' 'Follow me.' etc.)
– antagonism ('You are an idiot.' etc.)
– superiority ('I am superior to you.' etc.)
– query ('What do you want?' 'Can I help you?' etc.)
– salutation ('Hello!' etc.)
– rejection ('Go away!' etc.)
– directional ('It's that way.' etc.)
Morris says that all the people who interpreted the 'head toss' in these ways were wrong! In every case, he says, they

thought he was doing the 'head toss' in their local way . . . and he wasn't! There was always a slight difference. For example, the 'head toss' which means 'Come on' is usually done with a slight twist or turn of the head. Notice in the drawings below that the expression, the type of face and the clothing all contribute to other interpretations.

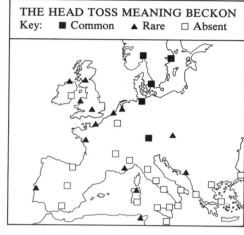

THE HEAD TOSS MEANING BECKON
Key: ■ Common   ▲ Rare   □ Absent

What does this position mean?

You are at a party of young people . . .

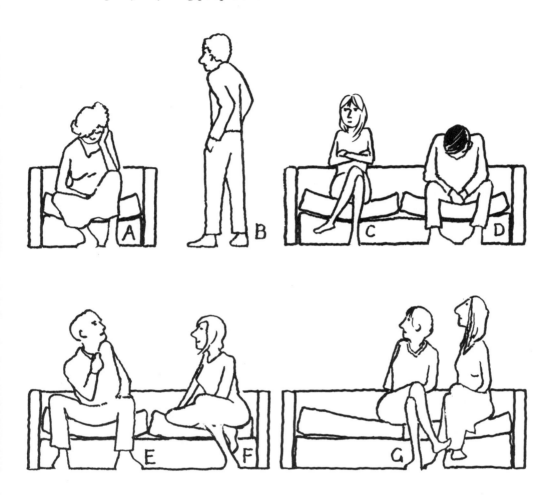

★ Match the actions:

1 This person is protecting him/herself. But he/she isn't frightened of his/her companion. They are talking about other people and sharing secrets. They are probably friends and have many interests in common.

2 This person is ready and open to do whatever is necessary! It isn't necessarily a threat, he/she just promises decision making and action.

3 This person is very interested and would like to impress someone but he/she isn't very confident. He/she has put his/her 'best foot forward'.

4 This person isn't very happy with his/her companion. He/she has 'closed him/herself off' from him/her.

5 This person is very interested in his/her companion. He/she listens to everything he/she says even if it is rather stupid! ⫸→

6 This person is bored by his/her companion and he/she doesn't care if he/she knows or not. In fact he/she rather hopes he/she will read his/her body language and go away!

7 This person really doesn't feel happy or confident at all. He/she would rather like to disappear so that he/she will not have to listen to his/her companion. He/she doesn't feel guilty about anything but very sorry about what is happening.

How did you know which person to choose for each description? What characteristics of the body positions communicated the feelings to you? Describe what communicates the information. Compare your answers with mine on page 83.

You are at a business occasion . . .

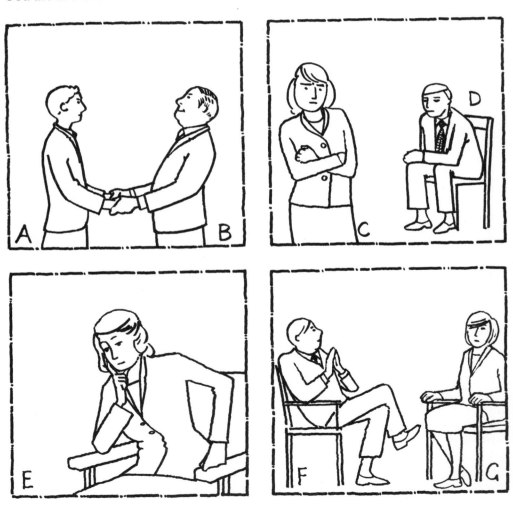

★ Match the actions:

1 This person is relaxed but ready to take action at any moment.

2 This person is thoughtful. And he/she probably thinks that the idea is a good one. He/she is ready to act when he/she has thought enough.

3 This person is very pleased to meet the other person. In fact he/she thinks the other person is rather important.

4 This person is very confident, he/she may even feel rather superior.

5 This person is determined not to move from his/her idea. He/she is angry and is only just controlling his/herself.

6 This person is determined to keep his/her self-control and stay cool and calm.

7 This person wants to show that he/she is an important person. At the same time he/she wants to make it clear that he/she wants to be 'nice' to the other.

See my answers on page 83.

Curtain up!

★★ Try these 19th century theatrical gestures. (See answers on page 84.) Do them and ask someone else what they mean.

First gesture:

1 Hold your left arm up in front of you. Now lower your arm slowly towards the other person.

2 As your arm comes down . . . slowly open your hand like a fan. Make your little finger point towards your chest. Turn your arm as you point your little finger.

3 Move your hand towards your chest and move your elbow outwards.

Second gesture:

1 Raise your shoulders. Show surprise on your face . . . open your eyes wide. Open your mouth. And raise your eyebrows.

2 Raise your left arm. Bend it and bring the ends of your fingers to your mouth.

3 Straighten out your left arm to the other person. At the same time keep the right arm against the side of the body. Keep the upper part of this arm against the body and now raise the forearm out to the side.

4 As your left arm becomes straight, bend your hand downwards so that your open palm is towards the other person.

WHAT IS SHE SAYING . . . WHAT IS HE THINKING?

These are theatrical gestures which were used during the last century.

★★ What do you think the man and woman might be saying? Fill in the speech and the thought bubbles.

Compare your answer with someone else's answer. (If you want to make a joke . . . put in the opposite of what you think she is saying or he is thinking.)

WHAT DO THESE GESTURES MEAN?

These hand gestures were used by actors in the 19th century. What did they mean?

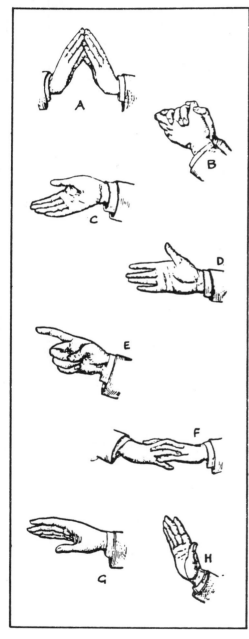

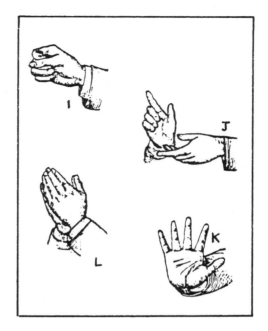

★ Match the actors' speech to the gesture:

1 'Please, please, my darling never leave me . . . or I shall die!'

2 'Never! How can you think that I would do such a thing!'

3 'I warn you, young man. If I find you doing that again I shall punish you!'

4 'Of course, my dear, help yourself!'

5 'Please be sensible! You must stop this stupid behaviour or you will lose everything!'

6 'I don't care what I do.'

7 'Get away from me you filthy, filthy beast!'

8 'Of course! Don't worry about it! I'll do it!'

9 'I will finish my work even if it kills me!'

10 'I don't agree with you. Now you listen to me!'

11 'Don't do it. Please don't do it!'

12 'Perhaps you would like to come for a little walk with me?'

(See answers on page 84.)

'She's a typical librarian!'

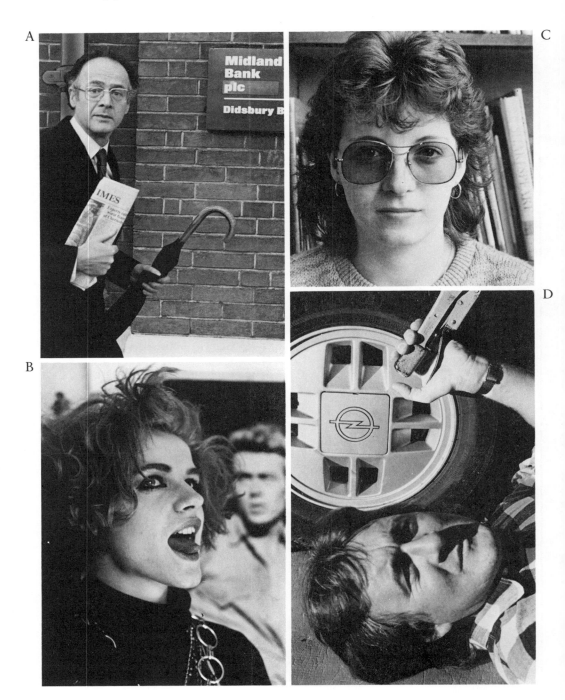

Here are four descriptions of the people in the photographs. Each description is a *stereotype* – a common and fixed idea which may not be true. For example, 'little girls are sweet and gentle'; 'little boys are naughty and cheeky'; 'fat people are jolly and happy and always eat a lot'. We often use stereotypes when we are talking in general terms.

★ Which stereotype do you think fits which person above?

1 This person is 'happy go lucky'! He/she is an architect and enjoys working on the building site more than in the office. His/her hobby is rugby football.

2 This person is training to be a librarian. He/she loves books and loves organising and arranging them. He/she doesn't have any special hobby or sport. But he/she does like to go out at weekends to visit old houses.

3 This person lives for parties, discos and nightlife generally. He/she only likes to think of music, the latest crazy fashions and his/her friends. He/she really doesn't like to think apart from that!

4 This person works in a bank. He/she is very serious and likes working with figures and official papers. His/her hobby is stamp collecting and he/she has a very fine collection.

(Suggested answers on page 84.)

BUT THESE ARE REAL PEOPLE!

I know all of these people very well and none of the stereotyped descriptions above belong to any of them! Below are four true descriptions of them.

★ Can you guess which description fits which person?

5 He/she earns his living by lecturing in art and design and by writing and drawing. He writes and tells stories and he loves riding on a unicycle and working with his friends who are travelling clowns.

6 He/she is a qualified pilot but not professionally employed as a pilot. He/she enjoys parachuting from planes and is also a marathon runner.

7 He/she is a doctor and sees hundreds of patients every week. He/she is a leading expert in helping people to stop smoking and has been invited to lecture on this subject in North America and Australia.

8 He/she is studying anthropology and the history of art. He/she enjoys reading and visiting old houses and archaeological sites. He/she does enjoy music and dancing as well!

(Answers on page 84.)

WHAT ABOUT YOU?

Are you a 'type' of person? Do you think that people look at you and say, 'Oh, I can guess what he/she is like!' What do people think when they see you? How much of this is true, do you think?

You have many experiences, thoughts and feelings which aren't shown in your face and body and clothes, and most people realise this. If we judge people by stereotyped ideas then we will often miss interesting and valuable experiences. In this way stereotyping is bad for good communication!

How to read a face

Our faces and our personalities

★ Try this. Answer these questions and then compare your answers with the answers of British people! (I showed these photographs to ten British people and asked them to answer the same questions. You can find out whether your judgements are similar or quite different, see answers on page 84.)

Questions:

Which person in the photographs looks . . .

1 The most artistic?
2 The most intelligent?
3 The kindest?

I asked the same ten people whether they really believe it is possible to judge someone's personality by studying their face. Do you think it is? Do you usually trust your first impressions? (You will find my survey answers on page 85.)

★ Study the six faces on page 31 and decide which description fits which face. (These descriptions were given by Pastor Lavater in the 19th century.)

1 unintelligent and conceited
2 happy, honest, intelligent and sensuous
3 talented but weak
4 unnatural and unhealthy
5 honest and thoughtful but too tense
6 nervous, delicate but intelligent

(For Lavater's interpretations see page 85.)

A

B

C

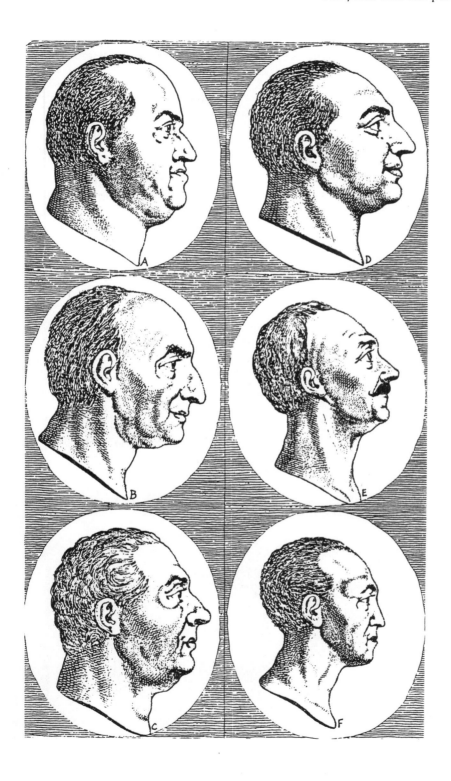

Now, if you think Lavater is quite right (and I certainly don't!) you might like to have some more advice from him:

'If you have a long, high bony forehead, never get friendly with anyone whose head is almost in the form of a ball. If your own head is almost in the form of a ball never get friendly with anyone whose forehead is long, high and bony.'

'Stay away from a man in whose face you have discovered anything however small, which you dislike, which appears as soon as the face shows any emotion at all, and which never entirely disappears. Be particularly careful if you do not like the mouth or the creases of the skin around the mouth; no matter what other outstanding qualities the man may have, you would always be on the losing side in such a relationship, perhaps even without being aware of it.'

'Stay well away from any man whose gaze and mouth are both unbalanced, and who has a broad, jutting chin.'

In a more recent survey, psychologists found that people who wear spectacles are thought to be intelligent, dependable and hard-working. In another survey it was found that people who wear glasses and do nothing for 15 seconds are judged to have 15 points over the average Intelligence Level (I.Q.)!

Will we really find a good friend by choosing the 'right' face?

Our faces and our expressions

A   B   C

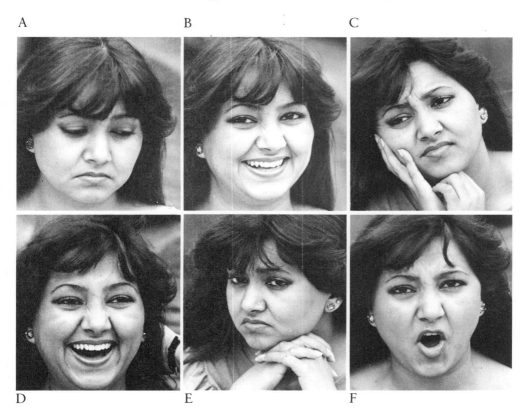

D   E   F

★ Match the words below to the faces. Only give one word to each face.

anger	happiness
joy	sadness
despair	boredom
pain	amusement
surprise	fear
loneliness	love
sympathy	disgust
delight	thoughtfulness

★★ Ask someone else to decide which words they would choose. Compare your answers.

Do you think you can judge people's feelings quite well? Would you like to have had more information before making your decision?

Are the seven emotions below easy to recognise? Can you always be sure?

People's faces are so important to us. Our earliest impressions are of our mother's face looking down on us. But we only learn a small amount of information from people's faces. We also learn how people feel from how they move, from what they say, and from the situation as a whole. And some people's faces are made so that they seem to be sad when the person isn't sad, or seem to be ugly and crude when they are creative and intelligent. Socrates, the Greek philosopher and one of the greatest thinkers of all time, looks . . . well, how do you think he looks?

Socrates. The Capitoline Museum, Rome

Perhaps we give too much importance to the face as a source of information.

Eyes: the windows of the soul

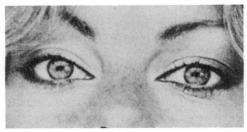

★ What do these English idioms mean? (You may know already, or you may be able to guess. See answers on page 85.)

A catch someone's eye
B have your/my/his/her eye on someone
C look someone straight in the eye
D can't take his/her eyes off her/him
E someone's eyes nearly/almost popped out of his/her head
F make eyes at

YOUR EYES AND YOUR PERSONALITY

If you look at other people's eyes a lot when you talk, people will think that you are open, friendly, self-confident, natural and sincere. If you avoid eye contact with people, they will think that you are cold and defensive, and they will think you don't really care about them or the conversation. And it may not be true!

Eye contact in different countries

Southern Europeans look at each other more than Northern Europeans and Americans. An Italian might think that an Englishman is cold and an Englishman might think that an Italian is very friendly! And it may not be true!

EYE CONTACT IN CONVERSATION

In an ordinary conversation between two people we spend about a third of the time looking at each other. The eye contact follows a pattern, it is like a dance! When we begin to speak to the other person we look at them. When we are sure they are listening we look away. Occasionally we look at them to see if they are still listening and understanding or agreeing etc. Then, when we finish speaking we look at them again. The listener looks at the speaker most of the time. If we don't follow this pattern it will communicate a special meaning!

Getting friendly!

When we start to speak we usually look at the other person for a few seconds and then look away. However, if we are very attracted to the other person we may continue to look longer than usual! If we have only just met the

other person then we will not look at them for too long because they may not like it. However, even a few seconds longer than normal will 'tell' them that we are specially interested.

Getting angry

We also begin to stare at the other person more when we are angry! They

know we aren't loving because of our 'hard' face, our narrowed eyes, our voice and our words.

Getting frightened

When we are a little bit nervous of someone then we don't look at them. We don't want them to look at us! But if we become frightened then we watch them with horror!

Hiding our feelings

It is easier to hide our feelings with our mouth than with our eyes. We can smile when we are anxious or not smile

35

when we are attracted to someone. But we forget our eyes! If we are attracted to someone, we look a little bit more than usual. Our eyes soften or look thoughtful to show our interest.

The pupil, the eyelid and the eyebrow

The pupil can become small because we are angry or it can become large if we are excited. Professional fighters, sales people and lovers are very quick to notice the change in the size of the pupil!

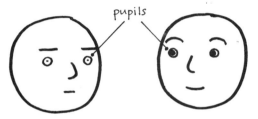

The eyelids communicate more than the eyes themselves. If the eyelids narrow the person is concentrating. (It is difficult to say whether the person is for or against the idea he or she is thinking about.) The eyelids may open wide with astonishment or with fear. If the person doesn't move his or her eyelids very much it means that they are calm and confident, e.g. 'He didn't bat an eyelid!'

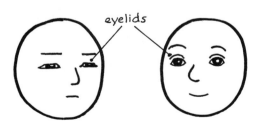

The eyebrows come nearer to the eyes when we are thinking hard, and

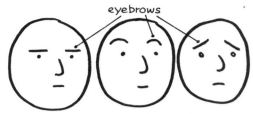

they come nearer together in the middle. It is difficult to know whether the person is angry or just thinking. The eyebrows rise when we are surprised. And when we are unhappy they come towards each other and, at the same time, rise up in the middle. Sometimes these movements are very small. Nevertheless they tell us a lot.

Children sometimes play the game of staring into each other's eyes. The first child to turn away his or her eyes is the loser. It is very hard to stare at someone unless you are very angry or very much in love. The eyes are the 'window of the soul'. Through the eyes we feel the enormous presence of another person. And that is something which is rather frightening.

How to use space

The Englishman's home is his castle

People often say that the Englishman's home is his castle. They mean that the home is very important and personal. Most people in Britain live in houses rather than flats, and many people own their homes. This means that they can make them individual; they can paint them, and change them in any way they like. Most houses have a garden, even if it is a very small one, and the garden is usually loved. The house and the garden are the private space of the individual. In a crowded city the individual knows that he or she has a private space which is only for him or herself and for invited friends.

People usually like to mark their space. Are you sitting now in your home or in a library or on a beach or a train? Have you marked the space around yourself as yours? If you are on the beach you may have spread your towels around you; on the train you may have put your coat or small bag on the seat beside you; in a library you may have spread your books around you. If you share a flat you may have one corner or chair which is your own.

Once I was travelling on a train to London. I was in a section for four people and there was a table between us. The man on the opposite side to me had his briefcase on the table. There was no space on my side of the table at all. I was annoyed. I thought he thought that he owned the whole table. I had been reading a book about non-verbal communication so . . . I took various papers out of my bag and put them on his case! When I did this he stiffened and his eyes nearly popped out of his head. I had invaded his space! A few minutes later I took my papers off his case in order to read them. He immediately moved his case to his side of the table. (Of course, it is possible that he just wanted to be helpful to me!)

If you are visiting another country you may feel that you don't have any private space. Hotel rooms look much the same in every country in the world. All day long you share public spaces with other people. You see the local people in their private spaces and you feel alone and 'outside'. Local people can create their private spaces by talking about things you don't know about. They wear clothes or symbols of clubs you can't belong to. They laugh and talk and exclude you, and even if they turn to you sometimes and ask you a polite question you know you are 'outside them'. And you even feel that they like you to be outside them so that they will enjoy being inside even more! This is one of the difficulties of being a traveller! But if you understand it then it helps you. Haven't you enjoyed being part of a group and 'owning' a bit of space?

Talking, sitting and standing

If someone is standing up he or she is a little more important than someone who is sitting down. (Unless they are separated by a desk.) Psychologists say that we like visitors to sit down so that we can dominate them!

Officials, office managers, etc. usually

like to sit behind a desk. Only their superiors can walk behind the desk and talk to them. If the official wants to be nice to us then he or she may come from behind the desk and sit down with us in a different place in the room. He or she is saying, 'Look, I am a reasonable person. I am prepared to leave my position of power. But I expect you to co-operate with me.'

People prefer to sit next to the other person or at right angles. If people sit opposite each other they fear the conversation will become too personal. Or they may feel that they will begin to argue and oppose each other.

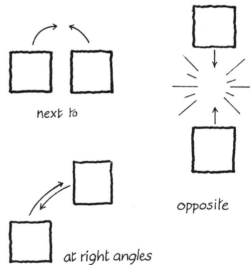

next to

at right angles

opposite

Give me elbow room!

An American psychologist has studied the distance between people in North America when they speak to each other. Here are some of the interesting facts which he found:

An American male from the North-East of America stands 50 cm away when he talks to a man he doesn't know well. If he talks to a woman he doesn't know well he stands 60 cm away. If males stand as near as 20 cm to 35 cm away from each other it is either because they are very aggressive or unusually friendly. And yet in many parts of South America or the Middle East people stand very near to each other. It is very difficult for a South American to talk to a North American! For the South American it is as if he is having to talk to someone in the distance; he would like to stand much closer.

Some general guidance for visitors to North America and Britain

From touching to 50 cm: We don't like people to come too near to us. Only close family and lovers can come so close.

50 cm to 1 m 20 cm: Our friends can come within this space.

1 m 20 cm to 2 m 70 cm: All the other people that we meet usually come within this area.

Over 2 m 70 cm: This is public space. We don't feel that it belongs to us.

Behind us: Strangers can come much closer behind us if they stand with their backs to us.

CROWDED PLACES

Of course, if we are in a crowded place we accept that people must stand very close to us. On the bus or the underground, in the rush hour, people may press against us. We all accept this. We accept it because we can see the reason for it. However, if the underground is nearly empty and someone stands next to us then we will feel uncomfortable.

An American psychologist studied this behaviour: he sat down next to people in a park when there were other empty seats nearby. In most cases the other people got up and walked away!

If we have to stand or sit in a crowded place then we pretend that the other people aren't really there: we don't look at them, we try not to touch them and we show an expressionless face.

In a crowded cinema we may be annoyed by the person next to us; he or she may want to take all the arm rest between us! But when the show starts we forget about it because we concentrate on the performers who are far away.

So what does it mean if someone stands or sits or is close to us or far away? Each of these factors is part of all the information we receive and part of the situation as a whole. We can't interpret any single bit of information separately from everything else.

Do you touch people?

Many Northern Europeans and North Americans don't touch each other very much. How often do you touch other people? How often have you touched other people today? What sort of touching was it? What did it mean? And where do we touch each other? Compare your attitude to touching with the attitude of most Northern Europeans and North Americans described here:

The psychologist Jourard showed three hundred college students in the United States a drawing of a person (see opposite). The person was divided into 12 parts. The students were asked:
1 Who touches you? (your mother, your father, friends of the same sex, friends of the opposite sex?)
2 How often do they touch you? (frequently, quite often, rarely, hardly ever?)
3 Where do they touch you?
★ How would you answer the questions? You don't need to tell anyone!
You may like to compare your experience with the experience of North Americans.
– Mothers touch their daughters more than their sons on their arms and their hair.
– Mothers touch their sons more than their daughters on their chests.
– Fathers touch their daughters more than their sons on their hair, faces, neck and shoulders.
– Men friends touch each other more than women friends on the shoulders, chest and legs.
– Women friends touch each other more than men friends on the hair, face, neck and forearms.

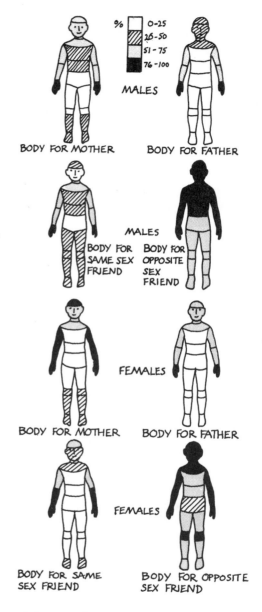

% 0-25
26-50
51-75
76-100

MALES

BODY FOR MOTHER   BODY FOR FATHER

MALES
BODY FOR SAME SEX FRIEND   BODY FOR OPPOSITE SEX FRIEND

FEMALES

BODY FOR MOTHER   BODY FOR FATHER

FEMALES

BODY FOR SAME SEX FRIEND   BODY FOR OPPOSITE SEX FRIEND

– Men touch women more on the knee than women touch men.
– Women touch men more on the chest and the hips than men touch women.
★ Which of these answers do you think are obvious and which do you think are surprising?

TOUCHING IN FOUR CITIES

Jourard did further research into touching. He sat in cafés in four cities and noted down every time he saw someone touch someone else. His notes were:

San Juan (Puerto Rico)   180
Paris   102
Gainesville (Florida)   2
London   0

Common touching and uncommon touching in the West

★ Which of these types of behaviour would surprise or shock someone from another part of the world?

Shaking hands

People who are very good friends don't shake hands. (Unless they haven't seen each other for a long time or one wants to congratulate the other.)
People can give a warm handshake by:
– squeezing your hand hard
– shaking your hand with both of theirs
– shaking your hand and then patting you on the back or even hugging you with the other arm

Many people would like to hug other people but feel they shouldn't do so. They show that they would like to hug you because they lean forwards a little bit when they shake your hand.

As a foreign visitor to Britain and the States, people will shake you by the hand when you are introduced and when you finally depart. They will probably not shake your hand at other times.

Patting

Some British and American people would like to hug you but they feel they shouldn't, so they pat you instead! They should only pat you on the arm, hand, shoulder or back. If they pat you anywhere else then it means more than general friendliness!

Linking arms

Two (or three) women sometimes do this. It is simply a friendly sign. Women sometimes link their arms through the arm of their male companion; however, this is becoming less common.

Shoulder hold

It is quite common for a young man to put his arm round the shoulder of his girlfriend.

Holding hands

It is no longer very common for young lovers to hold hands.

Holding the waist

This is more serious than holding someone's shoulder!

A *full hug*

It is quite common to hug a much-loved friend or relation if he or she has been away for a long time.

Kissing

In some countries it is quite common for men to kiss each other as a greeting. In Britain and North America it is rarely done. Women sometimes kiss each other. In some families it is very common to kiss as a greeting, but in many families it is never done. Hugging and kissing between lovers in public is acceptable but not common.

A *tip for a visitor to Britain or North America*

You can see from the descriptions above that people don't touch and hug each other very much in Britain and North America, but this doesn't mean that the people aren't warm and don't like each other . . . and you!

And, of course, if other people's behaviour seems strange to you then yours will seem strange to them. But behaviour is language and we all have different ways of expressing ourselves. Body language is not an international language.

How to recognise the roles people play

An introduction to roles

We all want to say at some time or another that we would like to have a drink, that the post office is in the second street on the left and that we don't like the latest pop tune. Conveying and exchanging information and opinions of this kind are very necessary. However, we are also concerned about our relationship with other people.

Sometimes our relationship is chosen by what society expects: if we are a host then we expect to do and say certain things. Correspondingly, other people expect us to behave in a certain way and they think of us as 'the host'. There are many other obvious roles: boss, servant, customer, teacher, parent, young person, etc.

As society changes so does the way in which these roles are played. What we expect of a host, guest, teacher or student is not the same today as it was a hundred years ago. And there are clearly differences between what different individuals feel about roles. One individual will do and say things as 'host' which are not the same as someone else.

But individuals go beyond this personal playing out of social roles. We all play other, more personal roles as well: roles in which we are determined, or uncaring, or failures, or funny. We often play these roles deliberately in order to manipulate the situation we are in and to get something from the people we are with. Successful communicators understand the importance in themselves and in others of these personal roles. They know how to respond to other people in order to reach an understanding.

The greater part of this section is about personal roles; the last part of the section is about social roles. The ideas described here are based on a popular school of psychology which began in the 1950s and is particularly associated with the work of Eric Berne. I have found the ideas of this school useful in communicating with people. At the same time they don't exclude other ways of studying people and how they behave.

Three people in every person

We all have three people within us. One of them is an *adult*, the other a *parent* and the third a *child*.

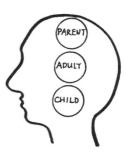

The *parent*: when the *parent* in our head controls us we correct people, we tell them how to behave as our parents told us to behave. The good side of *parent* is caring for people and passing on the traditions of society. The bad side of *parent* is giving more importance to traditions and rules than to the needs of the individual.

The *adult*: the *adult* in our head looks carefully at information and tries to think of sensible ideas. Our *adult* is open-minded to new situations and to other people and their feelings and opinions. The good side of *adult* is thoughtfulness and openness to new ideas. The bad side of *adult* is not making decisions quickly and not giving importance to enjoyment, etc.

The *child*: everybody has a *child* within them. The *child* in each person is perhaps more important than the *adult* and the *parent*! The *child* gives us joy, openness, invention and activity, just like a child in a family. Unfortunately the *child* inside us is often not allowed to contribute . . . we are ashamed of having fun and being creative when we are older. And sometimes the *child* inside us is not healthy and we are 'childish' and silly and not 'child-like' and joyful, open and creative. The good side of *child* is joy, excitement, openness to new experiences and creative energy. The bad side of *child* is being silly, selfish, spoilt and conceited.

Everybody has these three people in their heads. Older people have a *child*

inside them and young people, even children, have a *parent* and an *adult* inside them! It is important that there is a balance of the good aspects of *parent*, *adult* and *child* within us. In this way we can be caring, thoughtful and joyous. The following section gives some ideas on how to recognise which of the three is in control both in us and in other people.

YOU SHOULDN'T PICK FLOWERS IN THE PARK!

DO YOU THINK IT'S EXPENSIVE?

HI! IT'S GREAT!

How to recognise a parent

What does a *parent* do and how does he or she behave?

NEVER DO THAT AGAIN!

head shaking!! to mean, 'No'.

eyebrows together to show anger

mouth small to show control of anger

chin raised to show superiority and determination

THAT IS STUPID AND UNACCEPTABLE TO ME.

YOU REALLY OUGHT TO START JOGGING.

raised chin to show determination

folded arms to show control

finger wagging to mean 'No' and 'Never'.

tapping foot to show impatience

hand on shoulder to mean 'I'm looking after you.'

Everyone can add other more individual types of *parent* behaviour. What do (or did) your parents do which is characteristic of them? Do you behave like your parents?

'Always', 'never', 'must', 'should' and 'ought' are important words for parents. These five words pass on traditions of behaviour. And these traditions aren't questioned. 'How many times have I told you?' 'If I were you I . . .' (can you think of an ending?) Words which give value either for or against something or someone are often *parent* words if they are based on traditional beliefs rather than on individual thought e.g. 'stupid', 'naughty', 'ridiculous', 'lazy', 'you poor thing', 'never mind, you'll soon feel better'.

How to recognise an adult

What does an *adult* do and what does he or she look like? There is no typical action of an *adult* except, perhaps, listening and looking thoughtful.

Questions are important for the *adult*: 'why', 'what', 'where', 'when', 'who', 'how', etc. And language can show when the *adult* is not sure: 'might be', 'could be', 'possibly', 'probably', etc. Also, language can show that the *adult* is more concerned about individual opinions rather than traditional beliefs: 'in my opinion', 'I think . . .'

How to recognise a child

Unlike the *adult* there are many physical clues to help us to recognise the *child*.

The *child* is the centre of his or her world and 'I' and 'me' and 'mine' are therefore very important. These words are often used with: 'want', 'wish', 'don't care'. And the *child* needs boasting words to seem important: 'big', 'bigger', 'biggest', 'lots of', etc. The child also uses words to express joy, energy and creativity: 'let's', 'lovely', 'beautiful', 'horrible', and language to express curiosity.

Can you recognise the parent, the adult and the child in yourself?

1 Can you remember one thing which one of your parents did and which you do now?
2 Can you remember one time today when you acted like a *parent* with someone?
3 Can you think of one situation today in which you were reasonable, you thought about the 'problem', you remained calm and you made a sensible decision?
4 Have you been a *child* today?
5 Do you think that when you are a *child* you behave as you did when you were about eight? Can you recognise any similarities?

Don't get your lines crossed!

have/get one's lines/wires crossed
colloq. to be mistaken about what someone else means or wants: *Your work's
good, but it's not exactly what your boss
is expecting – I think you two have got
your lines crossed somewhere.*

Two people can be *parent* to *parent*
with each other, for example, when
they share anxiety about the future of
their son or daughter. They can be

adult to *adult* with each other, for
example, when they discuss their
child's character and concerns and
decide how to advise him or her. They
can be *child* to *child* with each other,
for example, if they express and share
their joy. And they can be *child* to
parent with each other, for example, if
one person expresses anxiety and the
other advises them about what they
should do.

All of these relationships can be happy
ones . . . the lines between them are not
crossed!

The *parents* in these two people are
sharing their feelings and expressing
their sense of duty.

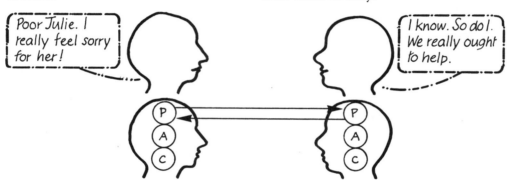

The *adults* in these two people are
exchanging information.

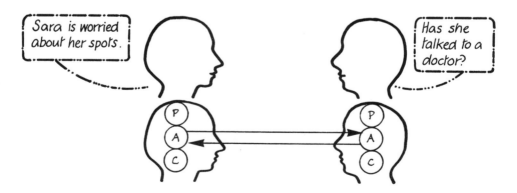

The *children* in these two people are
expressing how much they are enjoying
what they are doing.

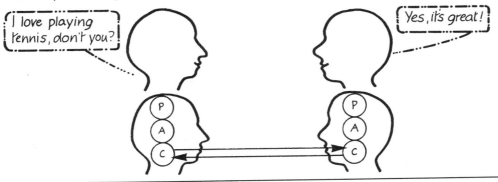

The *child* in the first person is
expressing his or her anxiety. The

parent in the second person is
instructing the *child* in the first person.

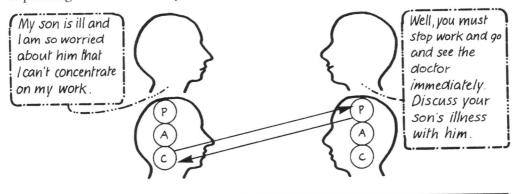

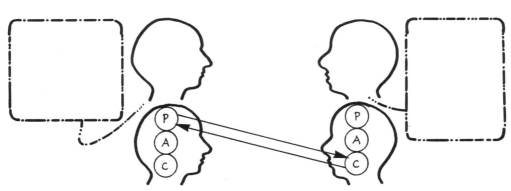

★ Try to imagine an exchange between
'a criticising *parent*' in one person

and 'an unreasonable *child*' in
another person.

If you get your lines crossed you will be in trouble! Your marriage, your friendships, your work with colleagues may all be damaged if you don't use the correct 'you', i.e. your *parent*, your *child* or your *adult*. It is not just the words we use which show whether our *parent*, *adult* or *child* is speaking, it is the way in which we speak. Imagine the sound of the voices in the examples which follow. In fact, some people deliberately use the words, for example, of an *adult* but use the tone of voice of a *parent* and that can cause trouble!

★ Imagine the next line after each of the bits of conversation below!

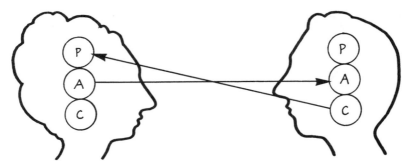

The *adult* in a woman speaks to the *adult* in her husband . . . BUT the *child* in the husband speaks to the *parent* in his wife!

Wife as *adult*: Could you do some shopping for me on the way home?

Husband as *child*: How can I go shopping? I won't finish work today until about six and then I'll probably have to go and have a drink with the boss!
Wife:

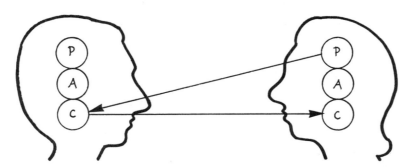

The *child* in a young man speaks to the *child* in his girlfriend . . . BUT the *parent* in his girlfriend replies to the *child* in him! Although their lines are not crossing they are not parallel! There might be trouble!

Boyfriend: Hey! I know. Let's see if we can cross that stream without getting wet!
Girlfriend: That's silly! What if you do get wet?
Boyfriend:
Girlfriend:

Things aren't what they seem to be!

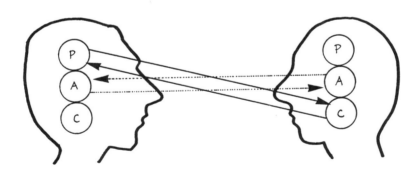

A car salesman says to the customer, 'This is a marvellous car – of course, it's a high quality car and it may be a little too expensive for you.'
What he says may be true. It seems as though his *adult* is talking sensibly to the customer's *adult*. If the customer's *adult* hears the salesman, he or she may say, 'Actually, you are probably right.' But if the *child* in the customer hears the salesman, he or she may not want to admit that they can't afford the car and say, 'The cost isn't important. I want a good quality car.' He or she seems to be replying like an *adult* but is really replying like a *child*. The salesman has succeeded, he has sold the car to someone who can't really afford it!

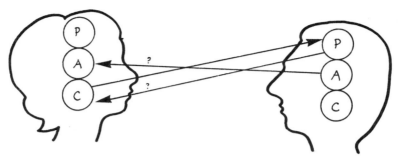

If a student is often late for classes or is careless with her work then she is 'inviting' the teacher to be a *parent* and criticise her. She appears to be a student who is attending a serious class but she is really behaving like an irresponsible *child*. If the teacher behaves like a *parent* then the student is pleased and will boast about annoying the teacher and complain about authority. If the teacher refuses to behave like a *parent* but behaves like an *adult* and asks the student how she feels about the lessons and whether she wishes to continue with them the student is in a difficult position: she may feel she has to respond with *adult* responsibility. Or the *child* in her may continue to behave irresponsibly until the *parent* in the teacher takes over from the *adult*!

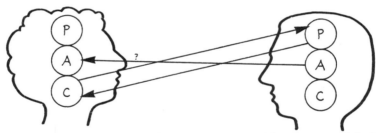

People often seem to be proud of doing something which is dangerous or silly. For example, a person may be proud that he has driven in a very short time from one town to another or he may be proud of drinking a lot of alcohol.
'I only took an hour and twenty
  minutes to get to Birmingham from
  Manchester!' (a car journey which
  usually takes about two hours or
  more)
'We must have drunk about ten pints
  last night!'
People like this seem to be describing a true incident as an *adult*. In fact their *child* is speaking. They either want the other person's *child* to respond with admiration or envy or they want the other person's *parent* to respond and be nice to them or reprimand them.
Admiring *parent*: What a fast driver
  you are!
Critical *parent*: You should be
  ashamed of yourself!
A *parent* or *child* response will encourage them to continue with the same sort of unsociable behaviour.

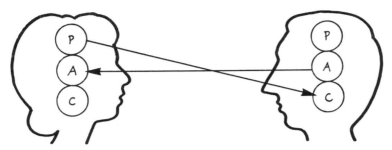

It can be difficult if 'things are not what they seem to be' when you are a visitor in someone's house. The host may seem to be an *adult* with you but really be a *parent*. And you may want to have an *adult* relationship with him or her. For example:

Host as *parent*: Now, while you are here you must go and visit the Roman ruins and, of course, you mustn't miss the old gatehouse where the city walls used to be.

You as *adult*: You feel they are very important? Perhaps you could tell me why they are important because I won't be able to see and do everything I want to during my stay.

If your host wants to treat you like a *child* and you insist on behaving like an *adult* there could be trouble!

What sort of game do you play?

Eric Berne used the word 'game' in his book, *Games People Play*, in a new way. For Berne 'game' means the way we want to affect other people and what we want to get out of it. The five 'games' described below are based on Berne's ideas. The *child* or the *parent* in us might play any of these 'games', but the *adult* in us never plays Berne's 'games'!

I'm no good at anything really

'I'm no good at anything really. Everything I do goes wrong. I've got a lousy job but I don't seem to be able to get another one. I don't have any interests because I'm not really good at anything. I don't seem to make friends like other people.'

Players of this game have found a simple answer to the problems of life . . . they always fail. They don't want to succeed because it would make their life more complicated; they would have to be more responsible. And players of this game often play the next one as well or enjoy the company of people who play the next one.

They are no good

People can hide their own self-criticism if they criticise others. 'He's useless. She's hopeless. He's just bad through and through. She is, quite frankly, a liar. He's from a rather inferior family. They always cheat you. You just can't trust them. He's lazy. She's not got a thought in her head.'

And to play this game successfully they must find someone who wants to play the first game! People who think they are failures are delighted by people who can 'prove' that society is filled with the corrupt, the deceitful and the ridiculous. Such claims make them feel justified in their own failure . . . 'How can I succeed when everyone around me is so bad/ridiculous?' etc. People who play the 'They are no good' game get their satisfaction from the attention of the first group.

I'm only trying to help

The person seems to want to help. But he or she is really expecting (and even wanting) their help not to be accepted. Then he or she can seem to be 'good' and, at the same time, badly treated. So they have two rewards, admiration and sympathy. 'I was only trying to help. If you don't appreciate my offer then I won't bother you any further . . . Some people don't appreciate help. He hadn't got the decency to say thank you after all I had done for him . . . She is an ungrateful little wretch.'

Be careful of this game if you are a visitor to someone's home! If your host offers you too much food and insists that you eat it; and insists on taking you to places which don't interest you; and insists on talking to you late at night when you are exhausted and want to go to bed; and insists on being with you all the time when you would like to be alone . . . then you are in a difficult position! If you refuse this 'kind hospitality' your host/hostess may play the 'I'm only trying to help you' game.

If only I wasn't so busy

'If only I wasn't so busy I would write a novel/work for the poor/spend more time with my family/lead a healthier life/do my work better.'

People who play this game seem to be so reasonable. And yet they always have an excuse for not doing something or for doing it badly. They expect praise for being so busy and sympathy for not being able to do what they really want to do. And they expect gratitude or compliments if they do do something!

To play this game successfully they need someone who thinks they are a failure. The 'failure' says, 'You are marvellous, I don't know how you find the energy.'

Sweetheart

The person wants to criticise the other person but doesn't want to quarrel. 'You do seem to upset people, don't you sweetheart?' It is difficult to quarrel with someone who calls you sweetheart! For this game to be successful the other person must disagree strongly. Then the first person wins! He or she has shown how unreasonable the other is! Instead of saying sweetheart the player might just use a soft and kindly voice or put his or her arm round the other person.

The player's aim is to avoid self-criticism through criticism of others. They also want people to say they are kind even though they don't really help. And if the other person rejects them they can be indignant.

Kiss me? You must be joking!

This game can be played by a man or a woman. In the traditional version of the game the woman seems to be interested in the man. But when he shows that he has been attracted she turns away from him and she might even be indignant! She may get satisfaction from seeing that he has been attracted or she may get satisfaction from hurting him. If she finds a man who wants to play 'Kiss me?' they will both have a successful game.

Some men play a similar game to 'Kiss me?' Their game is 'You can love me but you can't possess me'. In this game the man attracts the woman. He enjoys her attention but he doesn't intend to lose his independence. And he may find a woman who wants to play 'Men are so cruel'. She will 'enjoy' being hurt because it will prove what she always says about men. She doesn't want to think well of men because that would make her life complicated. She would have to think of them as individuals.

★ Do you know anyone who plays any of these 'games'? Can you think of any other 'games' which people play?

Why are games important?

Games are important if you want to communicate successfully. Most people play games a lot of the time. But they don't know they are playing games. If you don't play the game they want you to play then you aren't going to get on. You may not want to play their game, but you may want to get on with them (you may have to get on with them if they are your host!). If you know they are playing a game it will help you to be more patient with them.

It's not always easy

Undoubtedly each individual forms his or her own balance of *parent*, *adult* and *child* and decides whether to play one of Berne's games or indeed no games at all. But it is very difficult for the traveller (or for someone meeting foreign visitors) to know whether the other person's behaviour is personal to them or simply part of the normal behaviour expected by their society.

Unfortunately, it is more complicated still! Within any one society there are many sub-societies! What would be normal and acceptable behaviour in one of them would not be normal and acceptable in another. Furthermore, it is possible for each person to belong to a variety of different societies. He or she will behave differently in each one. This is obvious if we compare the way we behave at home with the way we behave at work. Or, in some cases, the way we behave with our colleagues at work and the way we behave with them away from our work place.

This problem is highlighted if we stay in someone's home in another country. For example, it is quite normal in Britain to ensure that the guest has everything which is necessary but not to give the guest a lot of attention apart from that. A guest from a country in which it is traditional to give a visitor a lot of attention might feel badly treated in a British home: they might feel that their British hosts are not very hospitable. It may be that the British tradition emphasises general kindliness and informality towards guests rather than hospitality as a grand occasion.

Another area of difficulty might be the relationship between men and women in the society and in particular within the family. A woman visitor to a British family might feel that the woman in a British home is treated like a servant: other visitors might feel that the woman in a British family has an unacceptably dominant role.

These judgements are based on what is felt to be 'normal' and 'right' in society. It is, therefore, particularly difficult to judge the role of the individual and the 'game' he or she might be playing! However, I believe Berne's ideas are useful even when we go to another country if they help us to be aware that there is more to conversation than just saying where the post office is or which pop tune people like!

To be a successful communicator in any country a person must know how to be polite, how to have a 'pass-time' conversation and be able to understand the games that people play . . . but, more important than all of these, they must be open, warm and happy to share.

How to get on with people

How to be a good listener

When I first went to London as a student I sat alone during parties with my glass of wine. I hoped people would think that I was having great thoughts, and that someone might come up to me and say, 'Excuse me! I hope you won't mind my coming up to you like this, I don't want to interrupt your thoughts . . . but really, you are the only interesting looking person in the room! May I talk to you?'
It never happened!

Here is some advice if you would like to be a good conversationalist: be an attentive listener. Encourage others to talk about themselves. To be interesting, be interested! Ask questions that other people will enjoy answering. Encourage them to talk about themselves and what they have done.

Remember that the people you are talking to are a hundred times more interested in themselves and their problems than they are in you and your problems. A person's toothache means more to that person than a famine in China which kills a million people. A pain in one's arm interests one more than 40 earthquakes in Africa. Think of that the next time you start a conversation.

Diogenes, the Greek philosopher who is supposed to have lived in a barrel, said, 'The reason why we have two ears and only one mouth is so that we may listen more and talk less!'

Do you know how to get on with people? Do you ever feel shy? What situations make you shy? Do you sometimes feel as if you don't know how to interest and amuse people and have conversations with them? Do you search desperately in your head for

THE REASON WHY WE HAVE TWO EARS AND ONLY ONE MOUTH IS SO THAT WE MAY LISTEN MORE AND TALK LESS!

DIOGENES

something to say? Do people find an excuse to leave you as soon as they can?

Try listening! Here are some more recommendations about listening:

(A neighbour of mine talking about her child)
'One evening last week I was sitting with Hannah, and she said to me, "You are a marvellous mum!" And I said, "Why do you say that suddenly?" And she said, "Well, although you're always busy you always stop what you are doing to listen to me."'

(From *How to Talk your Way to Success in Selling*)
'You have to force your buyer to talk . . . to enter the conversation . . . if you expect to talk your way to a successful sale. The only way you can do this is to stop talking yourself and listen.'

(From *Hamlet*)
'Give every man thine ear, but few thy voice.'

Airline employees are taught how to listen to complaints. If they are able to show sympathy and to listen long enough the passenger's problem will begin to seem less important. Psychologists, counsellors and doctors

also know that listening is part of their job. If they listen with care and concern the patient may even solve the problem! They are professional listeners. Here is some advice they give.

Show the other person that you are listening. Look at them. Smile and nod quite often, and shake your head or raise your eyebrows if you don't follow what they are saying. Don't tap your foot because this will show impatience. Don't look at your watch unless you really have to know the time, (and then you should tell the other person why you need to know the time). If you show impatience then the other person will lose their confidence and you will lose the moment of friendship which they are offering.

A good listener has magic! A good listener has the ability to make people feel good, and is as valuable at a party as a good talker. But just listening isn't enough. One should listen intelligently by trying to find out what the other person would really like to communicate.

★ Look at these two short bits of conversation. What is the person really saying?

'I work for a small firm which makes shirts. They are high quality shirts, the sort that cost about £40. It's a good job, really, and it keeps me pretty busy. I was promoted to the job of export manager last year because the previous man retired. I suppose they couldn't find anyone else. I've never actually been abroad. I suppose it's a challenge. Funny position to be in really . . .'

The way the man says these things and how he moves and behaves will show what he is thinking. He may really be wanting to say how busy he is, how anxious he is, or how he feels very inadequate to do the new job. Another example:

'Oh, I live a very ordinary life really. Nothing much happens to me. I seem to spend all my time shopping, cooking, washing up, listening to other people's problems, not that I mind too much . . .'

This person is saying that their life is boring and that they have nothing to talk about. But they might love to talk about their children and in their descriptions show what their interests, their hopes and their difficulties are. It need not be boring. After all, many great stories are based on families.

Repeating what the other person has said

Of course, at some point, you have to speak. The other person will need reassurance, they will need to know whether you have understood, whether you care about what they are saying, whether you are interested, and whether you want to hear any more. One of the easiest and most helpful

ways of responding is to repeat the sense of what the other person has been saying. In the first example above, about the export manager, you might say, 'So you're very busy then. It's rather a lot for you to do.' And for the second example, you might say, 'Looking after people you love must take up all your energy.'

Repeating the main points of what the person has been saying shows that you have been listening, and the fact that you have bothered to speak about what they have been saying shows that you care. You might help the person by giving them a particular question to answer; it will show them that you are interested and they will probably get pleasure in answering your question. However, if you express an opinion on the subject you will be taking a more positive part in the conversation and a shy person is then likely to say less or even stop speaking altogether. (Of course they may enjoy a discussion or even an argument, but that is another thing.)

Encouraging and discouraging

Let us suppose that you are at a dinner party talking to a person you don't know very well. This person tells you that they have just quarrelled with their father. Which of these responses would you give?
– Ah well. Every family has its ups and downs! Can I get you a drink?
– That sounds rather upsetting. It must be bothering you quite a lot.
Obviously the person wants to talk about the unhappy situation. One of the responses will encourage this and the other will certainly not!

How to be a good conversationalist

In the last section it was suggested that you can get the other person to do all the talking. All you need to do is to show that you are interested. Often it is enough simply to repeat the main thing which the other person has just said or to describe how they seem to be feeling. However, you may want to do more than just listen and the other person may want you to make some contribution to the conversation! Here are some of the advantages and disadvantages of different types of question and statement.

Statements and questions

The following questions are fairly helpful; they invite the person to say what they want to. They are open questions.

'How does it feel to do your homework with all your family about you?'

'You've been here for a week. What do you think of it?'

The following statements do the same work as the questions, but they are less directive. The questions come from someone who is taking the initiative. The statements come from someone who is saying, 'I am just another person who is interested in you.' Sometimes a statement helps people to relax more than an open question.

'It must be difficult to do your homework with all your family about you.'

'You've been here for a week. Your head must be full of impressions.'

★ Can you think of statements to replace the following questions?

1 What are your plans for this next week?

2 How do you get on with your parents?

3 What do you do when your neighbours annoy you?

4 How do you live on such a small amount of money?

(For some possible answers see page 85.)

OPEN AND CLOSED QUESTIONS

Psychiatrists like open questions, as they feel that the other person will relax and share themselves rather than be defensive. Which of the following are open and which are closed questions?

It's great food, isn't it?
What do you think about the food?
What's the matter with you today?
How are things going?
Do you like being a salesman?
What's it like being a salesman?
Sailing is an expensive sport, isn't it?
How expensive is sailing?

Open questions are fine for psychiatrists, but if you, as a non-psychiatrist, only use open questions you might begin to annoy people!

THE 'AGREE WITH ME' QUESTION

'It's quite wrong, isn't it?'
'In my opinion contemporary art is just ridiculous. Don't you agree?'
'It's such a wonderful piece of music, isn't it?'
'You would like to visit the old castle, wouldn't you?'

There is nothing wrong with these questions, but they aren't a 'good listener's' questions. They wouldn't help a shy person to respond. If you use questions like these you won't encourage the other person to speak.

DOUBLE QUESTIONS

Double questions are often used when someone is trying to sell something. For example, 'Shall I come round to see you on Thursday evening or Saturday afternoon?' They are a way of controlling the other person. Or, you might be at a party, and the host might say, 'Now, would you like to sit next to Janet or Barbara?' However, you might not want to sit next to either of them! Double questions are often difficult to answer in the way you want to; they aren't usually very useful for the 'good listener'.

AGREEING AND DISAGREEING

If you want to contribute rather than ask questions you will have to take something that the other person has said and then:
– disagree with it
– half agree and half disagree with it
– say something else which it has made you think about
★ Imagine you are at a party and someone says to you: 'I do think books are incredibly expensive, don't you?' Which of these replies would you give if you wanted to disagree?
'I don't agree I'm afraid. A book is still cheaper than an evening at the cinema . . .'
'You are quite wrong! Books are cheap. Think how much they cost to produce and how much you get from them!'
'Expensive? Expensive to whom? I never buy them. I just borrow them from my friends.'
Which of these replies will lead to a lively conversation? You might have to think of individual people you know before you can answer that question.
★ Think of examples of disagreement, half agreement and something different which you might say if someone said one of these sentences to you:
'Unemployment is terrible.'
'I really love just sitting in the country on a warm summer afternoon.'
Were your responses serious or humorous? Think of an example of the opposite feeling.

61

A good conversation

A good conversation is an exchange in which each person responds to the other even if they don't agree with them. Ben Jonson, the English writer and philosopher, said, 'That is the happiest conversation where there is no competition, no vanity, but a calm, quiet interchange of sentiments.'
Do you agree with him?

Politeness and 'pass-time' conversations

Do you often keep away from other people?

Have you kept away from people today . . . perhaps for half an hour?

Perhaps you went for a walk by yourself at lunchtime or perhaps you told your colleagues at work that you had to go shopping, but really you wanted to be by yourself. Do you daydream when people talk to you? Everybody needs time for themselves, time to be alone and to relax. Some people need more than others.

But correspondingly everyone needs other people. Do you know anyone who keeps away from other people a lot of the time? Are they happy, do you think?

We often keep away from other people, particularly strangers because we don't want to be hurt or seem to be foolish.

Do you often exchange politenesses with people?

Here is a polite greeting:
The other person: Hello, how are you?
You: Very well, thank you. How are you?
The other person: Fine!
You: Good!

But let us suppose you gave a different answer to the other person's question:
The other person: Hello, how are you?
You: Well, it depends on what you mean. If you mean am I physically well, then I am, as far as I know, although it is difficult to be sure. Emotionally, I am tired out and really should take a rest. Professionally, things are going OK but . . . and then there is my family

life which has never been right since Grandma lost her cat.

In the second conversation your reply would upset the other person. After all he or she is not really asking how you are but just greeting you. In a polite exchange the other person expects you to follow a pattern which is well-known and acceptable.

There are various reasons for choosing either a short or a long 'pattern of politeness'. The reason for a longer pattern of politeness might be that you haven't met for a long time. Perhaps the other person has been away on holiday. They might expect you to ask them about it. They may not expect you to be really interested! They just want you to acknowledge them with a longer conversation.

You: Oh, hello, John.

The other person: Hello, Mike.

You: It's nice to see you. You've been away, haven't you?

The other person: Yes.

You: Where did you go?

The other person: We went to Greece.

You: Oh, that's nice, particularly at this time of the year. Good weather?

The other person: Yes, fortunately. I needed it!

You: Oh, that's great. I envy you. Well, . . . must be going now.

The other person: Be seeing you.

You: Sure. Bye!

Successful communication doesn't necessarily mean exchanging information. It often means just 'being nice' to someone. Politeness and 'being nice' to people in this way are essential for all of us. However, some people never go beyond politeness. They never really want to know how someone feels or what they have experienced. They might be embarrassed if someone really told them. You can only get on well with someone who likes the same balance of politeness and real exchange of information as you do.

★ Re-write the conversation on page 63 so that one person only wants to be polite and the other insists on expressing the most individual and intimate details about themselves!

Do you talk to people just to pass the time?

(At a party with some neighbours)

You: Hello, Barbara, how are you? Have you got over that cold you had?

Barbara: Oh yes, fortunately. I couldn't have survived another day of it. It makes you feel so miserable, doesn't it?

You: And one looks so awful! My nose always goes bright red and my face even paler than usual so I look like a poppy on a plate.

Barbara: It's funny how some people never seem to get colds. Harry never gets a cold. He's never had one all the years I've known him.

You: Men! We look after them too well. Mind you it's a good job they don't catch colds so often. We would never hear the end of it. When John gets a cold you'd think he was dying. Men are pathetic when they are ill, don't you think?

If we are being polite with people there are only a few things we can choose to say. However, conversations which pass the time can be a little bit more varied. We have 'pass-time' conversations at parties or before meetings or when we are delayed in a train. Someone will choose a subject and comment on it in a general kind of way. And then someone else will add a comment. In a 'pass-time' conversation people don't show their individuality very much. Usually people agree with each other or only disagree in unimportant ways. And they don't try to start a serious discussion or argument which they care about.

'Pass-time' conversations are very important if you are travelling and visiting people's homes. 'Pass-time' conversations help you to get to know the other person a little bit. Then you can decide whether you want to get to know them better and to share more useful and interesting conversations. Here is a typical British 'pass-time' conversation. You can practise it!

The other person: It really has been awful weather in the last few days, hasn't it?

You: Absolutely terrible! We haven't really had a summer at all! / I suppose it's all right for the gardens. / It's just the time of year I suppose. / (and for the humourist) It's all right for ducks!

If you want to disagree, do so gently and in such a way that you don't upset them!

You: To tell you the truth I'm quite happy about the rain! I've just planted some seeds in the garden and it's just what they need. (If you just

made the statement, 'I'm quite happy about the rain!' and gave no explanation, particularly if you didn't smile, the other person would be offended!)

People sometimes talk about serious subjects in 'pass-time' conversations. And yet they don't really say anything which might be too original or disturbing.

★ In the 'pass-time' conversation below see if you can add the missing parts. Don't forget, don't be too serious and don't disturb the other person too much! I have given you a choice of sentences below. Choose those sentences which will make a 'pass-time' conversation which isn't too serious. And then see if you can make up a conversation in which one of you is being far too serious!

The other person: Pollution is such a problem these days, isn't it?
You:
The other person: Yes.
You:
The other person: Yes, I know.
You:
The other person: No.
You:
The other person: Bye then.

– Anyway, I'll have to be going now. Bye!
– I mean, people burned coal more than they do today and everything was really dirty. People were dying young of awful diseases because of the dirt.
– You know, the beach at the seaside is so often covered with plastic bottles.
– Anyway, I don't suppose you want to discuss things any further. So I'll be going now. Bye!
– Yes, so much is spoilt, isn't it?
– No, I don't really agree. It was much worse a hundred years ago.

POLLUTION? IT'S DISGUSTING!

– People shouldn't be allowed to throw their rubbish anywhere.
– People like you make these extraordinary statements. They don't help anybody. Of course, there is a pollution problem but it arises from the very nature of our society. We want things to be cheap and we don't want to spend extra money on keeping industry clean.

Of course, it is a problem if you don't want to have a 'pass-time' conversation about a subject which you care about. If you want to discuss the subject seriously then you may have to talk to someone else. But if the person is your host or sitting next to you on the train or the aeroplane what will you do?

In 'pass-time' conversations it doesn't matter if the conversation is interrupted. It isn't important anyway! At parties in Britain it is common for people not to sit down. They stand and talk, and this allows them to move to other people quite frequently. The excuse to stop the conversation is usually that you have to get some more wine. Sometimes somebody else joins in the conversation and then one of the first people can move away. And the next two can start up another basic

65

'pass-time' conversation. Of course, a 'pass-time' conversation can become a serious 'work' conversation in which people exchange useful, interesting and unexpected information. But then it is no longer a 'pass-time' conversation!

Here are three more examples of 'pass-time' conversations which might be useful for the foreign visitor to Britain:

The other person: They just don't seem to be able to run the railways like they used to.

You: I think it is probably the same everywhere.

You: The new Ford/Volkswagen/Austin Rover looks very nice, doesn't it?

The other person: It's all right but I prefer the Volvo/Toyota/Chevrolet myself.

You: What will they design next?

The other person: They've got to keep changing the fashion so that people will keep spending their money!

★ Here are some first lines from a chatty person who wants to start a 'pass-time' conversation with you. What would you say if you didn't wish to offend him or her?

1 'Children really are difficult on trains, aren't they?'

2 'Waiting in queues is not my idea of fun.'

3 'Things are so expensive these days, aren't they?'

How to start a conversation in Britain

Why do you learn a foreign language? To talk to people? Imagine you are in a railway compartment full of people, in England. You have been learning English for many years, and perhaps you have passed some examinations in English. You want to speak, but you don't know what to say!

Of course we are all different. We have different personalities, different interests and concerns. And, of course, it is often easier for two women to speak together than for a man and a woman. Some of these suggestions may therefore not be appropriate for all circumstances.

First of all, the other person will relax if you listen to them and respond to them. But sometimes the other person prefers to listen. They may not want to speak very much. In this case I think you should look at them when you speak, look into their eyes, respond to their changes of expression. If you do this they will know you are talking to them and not just talking about a subject.

But how do you begin? Usually, begin gently! Either make a statement or ask a question which is not too deep and personal. In Britain, the weather is always changing, so many people begin by talking about the weather. However, if you make an obvious statement they can only agree with you, and the conversation won't continue. So you must add a question. For example, 'It is rather wet at the moment. When is the best time to see England?' If you are in a foreign country, you might begin with a compliment. For example, glance at the person and then look at the landscape, (the harbour, some buildings, traffic, etc.) and say, 'The hills are so soft and everything is so green here. Is it like this everywhere in England?' 'What a delightful little harbour. I wonder what it is like to be a fisherman here?' 'The roads are very busy! I think the train is more comfortable, don't you?'

In each of these examples there is a question. It would be difficult to answer the question with 'Yes' or 'No',
as the question invites personal opinion and information. Of course, it would be possible not to ask a question at all: just to make one of the statements and then wait! However, you need to be brave and just hope that the other person will speak!

None of the questions above are about the other person. Usually it is better to ask about other things. When the other person talks about other things they show their interests, opinions and personality. Sometimes you can be more personal. If you compliment somebody and then show interest they may not feel 'attacked'. For example, 'Excuse me, but what a lovely bag that is. Did you buy it in England?' 'What a nice little dog you have. What sort is it? Do terriers have nice characters?'

Note that if people have a dog they will probably like you to say something about it. In Britain many friendships begin through people's dogs. The people don't look at each other and can restrict the conversation to the dog's eating, walking and sleeping habits and whether or not it barks at the television and likes a hot bath, for example.

Another approach

Why not say you are a visitor? Say that you don't understand a word, an idiom or some feature of local life. Ask the person to explain it to you. If they know that you are a foreigner they will probably feel responsible for you; they will think you know nothing and are not a threat to them.

Sometimes a conversation can start if you talk about yourself, as the other person doesn't feel attacked. If you give personal information about yourself they may feel they can do the same.

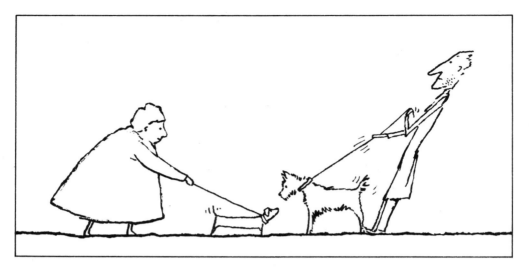

Of course, the other person may not wish to speak to you! They may want to dream, to relax, to read or do some work. They may think you are very boring! And of course, you must respect their wishes and feelings. But don't feel ashamed! You are not at fault. Conversation is sharing. I think that if we conversed more the world would be a happier place.

Are British people cool and reserved? It is true they may not talk as readily and as fully as, for example, many Italians. However, they are human! They like people to be interested in them and in their country so . . . be brave, speak to them. I really believe you will find it quite easy!

Conversational flowchart

Imagine that you are a visitor to Britain and that you are on a train. You would like to talk to an English person who is sitting opposite you. Look at the flowchart which follows. It shows several possible conversations. Notice how you would use open and closed questions, personal and impersonal questions, agreements and disagreements, statements and information about yourself, and requests for help.

★ Have a go . . . Try to make flowchart conversations which might take place at a dinner party, in a pub, when staying in someone's home, or with children in someone's home. Imagine that you are meeting the people for the first time.

you → It's a very full train, isn't it?

The other person... not very talkative.

Yes, it is.

Is it usually as full as this?·

I don't know. I don't travel on it very often.

The trains in my country are always very full / hardly ever full.

Oh, where do you come from then?

Sucess! You have made them ask a question!

Do you use this train very often?

Yes, I do.

Why is this train so popular, do you think?

Well, you can get saver tickets for this train.

What are saver tickets?

Well, you can get a cheaper ticket if .....

You've succeeded! They are talking at last!

I don't know why I chose it really. I could have come on an earlier one. Did you have to come on this one?

I did, actually.

Oh, what other ways are there of getting to London?

Well, there's the bus, of course.

What are the advantages?

Well, there's .....

You've got them going!

How to interest someone of the opposite sex

FIRST STAGE

If you try to attract someone of the opposite sex by the way you speak to them you are 'chatting them up'. Jean Goldsmith, the American psychologist, studied this very common human activity! She found, not surprisingly, that the first stage is a difficult one. Each person wants to be careful. They may not know each other so they don't want 'to give themselves away' too soon. And because they don't know each other they don't have much to talk about.

Here is an example of part of a 'first stage' conversation. The two people have started talking and then one says, 'Tell me about yourself.' How would you go on? Which of the following sentences might be the best reply?
'I'm not really very interesting.'
'You first!'
'Is there anything in particular you would like to know about me? I could tell you what I do for a start.'
During this first stage the actual conversation is perhaps not so very important. The two people will be concentrating on their body language! They may stand straighter or deliberately stand or sit in a relaxed kind of way. The man will probably expand his chest . . . the woman may do the same or move her legs in an attractive way. They might smooth their hair or re-arrange their clothes.

Gerald Clore, another American psychologist, has noticed a number of signals which a woman makes if she likes the man: she looks into his eyes, smiles broadly, makes movements towards him, touches his hand, uses expressive gestures while speaking and has 'wide open eyes'. A woman is uninterested if she gives a 'cold stare', frowns, looks around the room or at her fingers instead of at the man. An interested man looks into the woman's eyes, sits close and smiles a lot. (I think most people could have told Mr Clore this information!)

SECOND STAGE

Now you have decided that you like each other. You talk about what you feel and think about things. You talk about your fears, anxieties, the things you like and dislike about your family and personal details about your family, their strengths and weaknesses, etc. So perhaps you fix up a 'date' (an arrangement for a man and a woman to go out together).

In many societies it is the man who suggests the 'date'. He will make his decision according to the general feeling of interest and warmth, and he must guess at this interest from all the signals and information described above. Now comes an even more difficult moment for many people and particularly for the man who usually makes the decision to act! Now is the time for good communication!

When do they first touch each other? The man says to himself, 'Perhaps she is just friendly! Perhaps she doesn't want things to go any further?' What a terrible moment! (For some people at least!) According to some research in the United States half the men and women wanted to kiss at the end of a first date but nearly three-quarters of them expected that they would have to!

Although this book is called *How to Communicate Successfully* it can't give any more advice here . . . most people

have difficulties at this point!
Everybody has their own character
and personality. If someone learns a
technique which is not suitable for
their character they might attract the
'wrong' person! Perhaps, in this
human activity particularly, people
should concentrate on 'being themselves'.

How to argue

Do you really want to argue?

What do you really want? Do you want
the satisfaction of proving that the
other person is wrong and that you are
right? How will he or she feel if you
prove that they are wrong? They may
admit that they are wrong but they
won't like you for it. Does that matter
to you? It isn't pleasant to be disliked;
it isn't pleasant to dislike someone, and

co-operation is difficult when people
dislike each other.

If you feel that someone is wrong
and it is important for them that they
find out, then help them to find out for
themselves. Don't let them lose their
self-respect. Some people want to win
an argument because they want to win,
not because they are concerned with
the actual idea!

If you don't want to hurt the other person

If you want to make your point and
you really don't want to hurt the other
person then:
1 Listen to what they are saying:
both the obvious things and what
they feel.
2 Try to find out if there are things you
can both agree on, particularly
important things rather than details.
Keep on referring to the points you
agree on.
3 Suggest that you meet again once the
general ideas have been expressed.
That will give you both time to calm
down and to consider the argument
more fairly.
4 Admit clearly and readily when you
are wrong. Very few people will make
you suffer if you admit a mistake and
most will then do their utmost to be
constructive as a result. It will also
make them more ready to admit their
own mistakes.
5 Express through your behaviour as
well as your words that you respect
them even if you don't agree with
them. (The argument should not be
your personality against theirs!) It is
also important to express through your
behaviour that you are neither
aggressive, nor, on the other hand,
weak and full of false apologies.

Three ways of arguing

Aristotle said there are three ways of arguing: in the first you hope that people will believe you because they trust you (ethos); in the second you try to persuade the other person that you are right by being reasonable and referring to facts (logos); and in the third you try to persuade the other person by the strength of your belief and by changing their feelings (pathos).

ETHOS

Sometimes you can just make a statement and the other person will believe you. They trust you, perhaps because you have often been right in the past on similar things. Some people are trusted because they have an important job. Politicians want people to trust them, so they often behave in a calm, responsible way hoping that we shall believe them even though their arguments aren't very good. However, 'ethos' used to be a more powerful way of arguing than it is now.

LOGOS

Sometimes you need to argue your belief logically. You concentrate on your main belief and you must find facts which prove it. You shouldn't appeal to what someone else says or to tradition or to what a lot of people say they believe. Your facts should be a fair representation of all the facts and not a selection just to prove your case.

PATHOS

You argue passionately. You may refer to facts but really you are expressing your feelings. If you can express feelings which the other person shares with you then you will 'win your argument'. Emotional arguments are based on pride, fear, love, etc. They are the most powerful arguments of all and they have changed history. Whole populations have been persuaded to do dreadful things through the power of emotional argument.

ALL THREE!

Combine all three types of argument and you will be very powerful! Show that you are a person who can be trusted and has been correct in the past in similar arguments; show that your belief rests on facts and reason; express the passion with which you hold your belief and express it in a way that can be shared with your listener.

General advice

If you are arguing logically:

1 Be clear what your main belief is and don't forget it. It is very powerful when someone is clear and determined and won't be distracted.

2 Only use examples to illustrate your main point. Don't let the examples become important in themselves.

3 Choose examples which the other person knows or can imagine and understands in a similar way to you. It is essential to look for experiences that you share.

If you are arguing emotionally:

1 Have a clear feeling even if you can't name it.

2 Concentrate on examples rather than on general statements.

3 Choose examples which you know the other person has strong feelings about.

Some important points for thinkers and arguers

FACTS

'The sun rises in the East and sets in the West.' That is a fact which we can all accept today. People used to believe the earth was still and assumed the sun was moving. They therefore 'inferred' that

it went around the earth. Which of these statements is a fact and which is an inference?

– Jane is a calm sort of person.
– We need food in order to live.
– Steel is harder than wool.
– Doctors are intelligent.

We need to infer and generalise or we should never get anything done; however, we shouldn't confuse inferences with facts.

GENERALISATIONS

'It is generally cooler and wetter in England than in the Middle Eastern countries so it is advisable for tourists from those countries to be prepared.' That is a useful generalisation.

'Men are selfish.' 'Old people are simple-minded.' 'Students cause trouble.' How many more useless generalisations can you think of in two minutes? Generalisations like these stop people from being open-minded to individual experiences.

You can make a generalisation useful by adding a word like 'often' or 'sometimes' and then you won't annoy the other person but you will still make your point. 'Englishmen wear bowler hats' is a misleading generalisation. However, the following generalisations are reasonable: 'More men wear bowler hats in England than in most other countries.' 'Some Englishmen wear bowler hats.' 'A few Englishmen wear bowler hats in the City of London.'

Some people generalise from a single experience. For example, a visitor might visit your country and have an unhappy experience with someone. He or she may then say, 'The . . . are really very unfriendly. We are so much more kind and hospitable.' And even if someone had many unfortunate

experiences in your country it would be wrong of him or her to generalise. After all there are millions of people living there and even 20 bad experiences could be merely hard luck!

Generalisations often annoy a listener so that he or she becomes less interested in the points you are making. What sort of generalisations annoy you?

Generalisations are usually poor arguments in logical arguing although they can be powerful in emotional arguing.

HYPOTHESIS

A hypothesis is a belief. It isn't a fact. Your hypothesis may be based on facts but that doesn't make it a fact. There may be other facts which don't support your hypothesis. 'The nuclear arms race will lead to war.' That is a hypothesis, not a fact.

When you are arguing for your hypothesis you should concentrate on the facts and the relationship between them. Can you think of any hypotheses that people have said to you? Choose some which you don't agree with.

CRITICISING THE OTHER PERSON

Some people criticise the other person rather than the ideas they are arguing: 'You are too old to understand' rather than 'You are mainly concerned about your retirement and about your pension. And it is quite natural for you to want security. I am concerned about having lots of new experiences of the world.' If someone is opposing you it is very easy for them to attack you as a person rather than concentrate on your ideas. They aren't concerned with the truth, only with winning the argument.

SOME VERY POOR ARGUMENTS!

'Everyone says so.'
What an argument! People used to believe that the earth was the centre of the universe.

'The experts say so.'
It would be silly not to take the views of experts very seriously. However, experts don't always agree. The argument can't be won merely by quoting the experts. You still have to prove your point by reference to facts.

'It's just common sense.'
Some people say that they are just ordinary, sensible, uncomplicated people and believe in down-to-earth simple ideas. This claim makes them appear honest and clear thinking. It is an emotional appeal. They want to say something which is obviously true so that we will not argue with their actual belief which may be quite different.

How to protect yourself against salespeople

How many times have you persuaded somebody or been persuaded to do something today? Persuasion is one of the most important and common uses of communication. If we want to persuade someone to do something then we must understand them, we must try to understand their hopes, fears, plans, ambitions and values. Then we must offer what we want to 'sell' as an answer to their concern!

Salespeople are taught: 'Don't try to sell, show the customer why he or she should buy your product in order to achieve his or her ambitions!' Salespeople, public speakers, public relations representatives, etc. are taught how to approach you, how to behave, how to argue and how to persuade. We need to know what their techniques are in order to protect ourselves! And perhaps some of the techniques are reasonable for us to use when we ourselves want to persuade.

Professional persuaders are taught about people's basic needs for success

in work, love and respect, personal satisfaction, and survival.

How to observe the customer . . . YOU!

The salesperson is taught to:
– Observe you . . . how you dress, the car you drive, the possessions you have chosen, the way you live.
– Listen to you so that he or she can find out what you really want, what you feel and what you think is valuable.
– Decide which of these concerns are of most importance to you.

The salesperson is taught what to say to you

The salesperson learns how to find your main concerns and needs and he or she is taught the exact things to say to you. Notice that the salesperson always finishes with a question to which the customer answers 'Yes'.

Your wish for success

Salesperson: 'Frankly, this is a luxury car. It's for the person who needs quality and performance. Successful people are usually very busy people. They need reliability and an appearance which is appropriate to their responsibilities. I imagine these are important features for you, aren't they?'

Love and respect

Salesperson: 'It's a quality car and it has been highly praised in the press. I'm sure your family will be delighted by it as well, won't they?'

Personal satisfaction

Salesperson: 'It's a wonderful car to drive. It's a "driver's car". You'll appreciate the acceleration and the road holding; it's excellent at cornering. I expect that is important for you, isn't it?'

Survival

Salesperson: 'It's so well-made. It's guaranteed against rust for seven years . . . although it should be rust free for at least 20 years! It has a specially designed and made chassis which will resist damage in an accident. There are a number of safety features in the car which make it about as safe as it can be. There are so many bad drivers on the roads these days you have to be as careful as you can, don't you?'

ON THE TELEPHONE

Imagine that an insurance salesperson has phoned you up to suggest that he visit you and talk to you. You give two reasons for not wanting to meet him. He is prepared! His training book tells him exactly what to say in reply to your objections. Here are two examples. Notice that in each example the salesperson gives two alternative times when you could meet. He wants you to concentrate on 'when' to meet and not 'whether' to meet.

You say: 'I'm too busy.'
Salesperson: 'Perhaps I have suggested a difficult time, Mr Brown. Let me see if I can find a time which is better for you. Would you be free on Friday at say, eight o'clock? Or Saturday at three?'

You say: 'I haven't got enough money.'
Salesperson: '(*Smile*) Ha, ha, Mr

Brown, many people feel like that these days. However, you may be surprised to learn that you can begin by investing as little as £3 per week. In any case, all I am asking you to do is to see if we could be of value to you, if not now then possibly in the future. I have my diary in front of me: may I see you today at three o'clock or would ten thirty tomorrow morning be more convenient?'

THE QUESTIONS A SALESPERSON USES

Most people prefer to talk rather than to listen, and that is useful for the salesperson! The salesperson controls the conversation by asking questions. He or she can decide on the subject by asking the questions; this makes the customer think the salesperson is pleasant, interesting and concerned about him or her. At the same time the salesperson can find out what the customer wants and how to sell it to him or her.

The salesperson can sometimes use a direct question. For example, 'Would you like to sell your car in part exchange for a new one?'

The salesperson uses indirect questions when he or she doesn't wish to create embarrassment or annoy the customer. For example, 'What sort of price range have you got in mind?' (This means, of course, 'How much money do you want to spend?')

The salesperson uses open questions when he or she wants to find out what the customer feels and thinks and the reasons for thinking in this way. The questions may begin with 'What', 'When', 'Where', 'Why', 'Who', 'How'.

Limiting questions help to control the customer. If the customer is talking too much and beginning to decide not to buy, the salesperson interrupts with a question which makes him or her answer 'Yes' or 'No'. The customer won't be offended because the salesperson has asked a question, and will wait to see what else the salesperson wants to know.

IT ISN'T ONLY WORDS THAT SELL!

Here is some of the advice given to salespeople:

1 Don't stand too near the door when the customer answers it. He or she may think you are too aggressive.
2 When the customer has opened the door wipe your feet on the mat, if it is outside the door, and that will make the customer feel that he or she must invite you in.
3 Be smartly dressed and smile! You should look like a confident, reliable bank manager.
4 When you get into the customer's house take your overcoat off as soon as you can. This will show that you want to get down to work. But never take your jacket off: the customer might think you are too relaxed and impolite.
5 Wait until you are invited to sit

down. Never sit down in the customer's favourite chair!

6 Look around the room and find something to talk about.

7 Ask about the children and remember their names.

8 And for the car salesperson: Point at the various parts of the car with a good quality pen. The customer will then get used to the pen and will not get a shock when the salesperson offers the pen to the customer in order to sign the agreement.

THE IDEAL INTERVIEW

Here is an example of an ideal interview. It is written for insurance salespeople. YOU means the salesperson and HIM means you!

THE INTERVIEW

YOU 'Good morning, Mr Brown, my name is Gerald White. We have an appointment for 10.30.'

(*Don't* sit down until asked. If he doesn't take your coat, *ask* if you may take it off. Don't do business in your outdoor coat; and never take off your jacket – even if the heat is killing you.)

YOU 'Mr Brown, so that I may be of value to you, would you mind answering a few basic questions?'

(Take out your review questionnaire and complete it.)

(You should now have a good idea as to his needs – *GENTLY* – point out one or two and enquire if he is aware of them.)

(You are trying to establish a need and find the one most paramount.) (Having established the need you must now obtain the commitment.)

YOU 'Mr Brown – may I call you Terry? Thank you. Everyone knows me as Gerald. Terry – we have agreed you need to do something about . . . (the need established). So that I can show you a way of meeting your requirement/ need can you give me some idea as to how much you can set aside out of your present income right now that will not put a strain on your resources?'

(The commitment must come from him – don't tell him the minimum, it might be too little to meet his needs or less than he can afford.)
(If he is not sure suggest 3 or 4 different amounts, eg £25 per month, £15 per month, £50 per month, £35 per month – make sure the lowest figure is higher than the minimum to the plan you have in mind.)

HIM 'Well, I can afford £20 per month.'

YOU 'You're sure £20 per month is OK?'

HIM 'Yes.'

YOU 'It won't cut into your budget too much?'

HIM 'No.'

YOU 'Fine – I believe XYZ plan will do what you want. Shall we prepare an illustration? You said £20 per month was OK – I take it you mean £20 straight out of your pocket?'

HIM 'Yes.'

YOU 'Well, as we can add to that the tax relief, that makes it £23.53 per month – so you are already making a profit (SMILE) – that's good, isn't it? I said that was £23.53 per month – shall we round that off to £23 or £24?'

HIM 'Make it £23.' (He might say make it £25).

(Three times he has agreed to the commitment amount – you can now feel confident you got this right. It is of the utmost importance you do this – if you don't you may find at the end of your presentation he says he can't really afford it, then you are back to square one with little or no ammunition left to get the sale.)

YOU 'Terry, would you like to fill in the figures as I read them out from the rate book – here's a pen.'

(You need to keep him involved; if you fill it out he is sitting there with time to think of reasons for not going ahead.)

YOU 'Great – that's got the figures in – now let us go through the illustration again to make sure you agree this plan does what you want.'

(Explain the plan in full – make totally sure everything is understood – and now go for the close.)

YOU 'Right, Terry, let's get the paper-work out of the way.'

(Be ready with the application form. Ask each question and fill in the answers as he gives them.)

YOU 'Fine, will you now give me your signature here,' (point to the declaration). 'And here on the Standing Order/ Direct Debit. Now all I need is your cheque for the first net premium which is (85% of the gross – say £23) = £19.55 payable to (the assurance company).'

THE SALE IS COMPLETED

Salespeople are trained to make use of normal human communication! They are trained to listen to and to study the other person and to find out what is important to him or her. However, some people might say that salespeople don't use these techniques fairly. Do salespeople sometimes encourage our foolishness? Do we really need so many things? Have you bought anything recently which you didn't really need?

Were you persuaded by the salesperson or by being in the shop or seeing the shop window?

What are your main concerns, hopes, and ambitions which could be used by salespeople to persuade you to buy something? Do you feel that any of the salespeople's techniques described above can or should be used with friends or people that you know?

Last thoughts

It is natural for people to communicate. However, we must *learn* how to understand words, expressions of faces, gestures and actions. These 'languages of communication' are not natural in the sense that we are not born with them. They are different in each country, they are even different in each region and street and sometimes between families.

Successful communication means that the other person receives the message you intend. To communicate successfully you must understand the other person's needs, feelings and ideas as well as the way he or she uses language. So it is essential to study and listen to the other person.

At the beginning of this book I said that 'communicate' comes from the Latin word 'communicare', meaning 'to give' or 'to share'. For many people, 'communicate' means to persuade, control, and organise. Persuasion, control and organisation are certainly necessary in our society, but giving and caring are *essential* for society and for each individual. I hope that this book will make a small contribution to this broader meaning of 'communication'.

Answers

Your answers may not be quite the
same as mine!
1 Expressing feelings
2 Criticising behaviour
3 Greeting and expressing friendliness
4 Asking for directions
5 Asking about other people's ideas
6 Making suggestions

Page 7

Page 13

Reasonable answers would be:

A – 7, 3   D – 2, 8
B – 6, 4   E – 5, 10
C – 1, 9

Page 15

Here is one way of describing Haddon Hall to someone who has studied English for about two years. Do you think it is too difficult? Is your description very different?

'Haddon Hall is a very interesting old house. The oldest parts of the house were built in about 1100 by the Normans. The newest parts of the house were built about four hundred years ago in the 16th century. There is a room in the house called "the long gallery". It has a beautiful ceiling. Outside there is a rose garden. It's very beautiful and romantic. Be careful! It is so romantic that you might fall in love with the first English person you see! Then you will marry and not go home!'

Page 23

1 G   This woman (and indeed both of them!) is sitting with her legs crossed and that may mean that she is protecting herself. She isn't frightened of her neighbour, however, because she is sitting very close and leaning towards her.

2 B   He is ready for action, his legs are apart, he is on his toes, his hands are on his hips.

3 E   He isn't sitting in a confident and relaxed way; he is sitting on the edge of his chair. He is adjusting his tie nervously. He wants to show his interest and is sitting forwards but he isn't confident that he can sit forwards towards the young woman. He is putting one foot forward. In English we say that 'he is putting his best foot forward'.

4 C   She is leaning away from the young man, she doesn't really want to be with him. She has folded her arms to show that she is self-contained and doesn't want to open herself to him. She is lifting the toe of her foot and tapping it up and down. She is irritated and wants to show that she may not be able to control herself much longer.

5 F   She is looking at the man and turning her body towards him. She is showing that she feels relaxed in his company. She is obviously interested in him!

6 A   Her head is resting in her hand. (Notice that her hand is not in a 'thoughtful' position.) Her body is bent over, without a feeling of life.

7 D   He would rather be somewhere else! His feet are turning inwards as if he would like to hide in himself. He is leaning forward as if he would like to go. He is moving his hands one inside the other hoping that something will happen to save him!

Page 24

1 D   He is sitting down but, nevertheless, he is ready for action. He is leaning forwards and leaning on one arm which gives his attention a sense of direction. He has one hand halfway down his thigh and the elbow raised which suggests that he can stand up quickly. His head is raised with attention.

2 E   This is a thoughtful position with the head resting lightly on the hand. The forefinger is raised along the cheek to the cheekbone. The other fingers are curled away . . . they don't touch the mouth. If they touched the mouth she would be thinking but unsure of herself . . . but this lady is confident. She is attentive, notice the body leaning forward and the upraised arm.

3 A   He is leaning forwards to show that he feels that the other man

shouldn't bother to come towards him. His head is raised to catch every 'kindly' word.

4 F   He is holding his hands so that the fingers are together and raised in the air like a church steeple. This is a sign of supreme self-confidence, possibly arrogance. He is very happy for the other person to see how confident he is. His head is tilted backwards as well, and this makes his nose 'stick up'. We say, sometimes, 'He/she is very stuck up' meaning that He or she feels superior. He is leaning backwards with confidence but not in a relaxed way . . . he is ready for action. He has crossed his legs, which may show that he feels that, in spite of his confidence, he may need to protect himself.

5 C   She isn't facing the man. This shows that she doesn't want to be with him. She has folded her arms. This can mean that she wants to give herself self-confidence and protect herself. However, in this case it probably means that she is trying to control herself. Her hands are bunched into fists as if she would like to hit him! One hip is raised which shows that she feels she must continue to stand there although she doesn't really want to.

6 G   She is crossing her ankles. This often means that the person is controlling a strong emotion of some kind. Her body is held back stiffly against the chair . . . she doesn't look frightened of the man. Her hands aren't held together to give her comfort but they are gripping the arms of the chair, which suggests that she is holding back strong feelings. Her feelings may be of anxiety but are probably of irritation with the man and with herself because she doesn't know how to react to him.

7 B   Taking someone's hands in both of yours is a warm, comforting and friendly gesture. However, this man is leaning backwards and raising his head (and nose!) in a superior way. He is communicating two bits of information which are different! He is saying, 'I am superior but willing to be friendly.' This gesture is often used by politicians who want to get votes!

Page 25

First gesture: Attraction
Second gesture: Surprise

Page 27

1	B	7	K
2	G	8	D
3	E	9	I
4	C	10	J
5	H	11	L
6	F	12	A

Page 29

I think the following stereotypes and faces fit. Do you agree?
1 D   2 C   3 B   4 A
But these are real people!

The true descriptions are as follows:
5 A   (this is me!)
6 C   (this is one of my students)
7 D   (this is my neighbour)
8 B   (this is my daughter)

Page 30

Of the ten people I talked to:
Five thought A looks the kindest.
Three thought B looks the kindest.
Two thought C looks the kindest.
Six thought B looks the most artistic.
Three thought A looks the most
    artistic.
One thought C looks the most artistic.

Four thought C looks the most
intelligent.
Three thought A looks the most
intelligent.
Three thought B looks the most
intelligent.

Of the ten people I asked whether it is
possible to judge someone's personality
by studying their face for a short time:
Four thought it is.
Four thought it isn't.
Two weren't sure.

Page 30

Lavater's interpretations:
1 A   4 C
2 F   5 E
3 B   6 D

Page 34

Here are sentences which include the
idioms and help to give their meaning.
A He tried to catch her eye but she
   looked the other way because she
   didn't want to speak to him.
B I've had my eye on you for several
   weeks. So be careful!
C She looked him straight in the eye
   and said, with a determined voice,
   'It's all over!'
D She couldn't take her eyes off him
   all evening because she thought he
   was so handsome.
E My eyes nearly popped out of my
   head when I heard his amazing story!
F She made eyes at him so much that
   he felt rather embarrassed because
   his wife was with him!

Page 60

Possible statements to replace the
questions:
1 I imagine you have some plans for
the coming week.
2 It isn't always easy to get on with
one's parents.
3 It is difficult to know what to do
when neighbours are annoying.
4 It must be difficult to live on such a
small amount of money.

Acknowledgements

The author and publishers are grateful to the following authors, publishers and others who have given permission for the use of copyright material identified in the text. It has not been possible to identify the sources of all the material used and in such cases the publishers would welcome information from copyright owners.

The Sutcliffe Gallery for the photograph on p. 1; Ray Delvert and DACS for the photograph on p. 2 © DACS 1985; Popperfoto for the photograph on p. 3; Collins Publishers for the extract from the Collins *Gem Dictionary of Basic Facts on Computers* on p. 10; Jonathan Cape Ltd, Desmond Morris, Peter Collett, Peter Marsh and Marie O'Shaughnessy for permission to paraphrase an extract from *Gestures, their origins and distribution* on pp. 20–22; Archivi Alinari for the photograph on p. 34; The Consumers' Association for the extract from *Which?* on pp. 78–79. All other photographs by Bill Godfrey.